Contents

Tutor: It is often tiny seeds from your experience which will give you the key to the student you are working with. Kindness plus patience. The students are very demanding; in fact you have to sit there and *wait* for them to find it out. Things which were obvious to you and *easy* to you and to which you do not even give a second thought are very *new* to them. And this is something you have to work at.

Students: I was terrified when I took my (driving) test because I had to memorise everything – it's always with you, sometimes you notice it more than other times.

and: Well, I'm getting on very slowly with my reading – very slowly – but it's helping me in a sort of way, in myself.

and: If you get easier in your mind then you can do things. When you go out with others, you can still do part of it (reading and writing). You do not feel as if you have to stand in the background all the time.

The Concept of Success in Adult Literacy

A H Charnley and H A Jones

Adult Literacy & Basic Skills Unit

Acknowledgements

We wish to acknowledge the generous co-operation of officers, organisers, tutors and students in local authority and voluntary organisations; the assurance of confidentiality precludes a more exact identification of those to whom we owe so much.

We are grateful for the continuous empathetic and supportive interest in our endeavours shown by Rosemary Jellis, Margaret Peters and Jack Mezirow, and we are also mindful of our debt to George Low who shepherded our manuscript to the printers.

Typography by Leslie and Lorraine Gerry

First published 1979 by Huntinton Publishers Limited

Published 1981 & 1986 by The Adult Literacy and Basic Skills Unit, Kingsbourne House, 229/231 High Holborn, London WC1V 7DA. Tel: 01-405 4017.

Reprinted August 1987

Introduction

The Adult Literacy Campaign is regarded as one of the most important developments in adult education in the United Kingdom. It is unique, in the sense that adult literacy has been found to be a problem in a developed industrial society where all adults under the age of 65 received at least eight years of compulsory education. This book is about the aims and achievements of students who came forward, and of their tutors, and records, mainly in their own words, their perceptions of adult literacy.

To understand the concepts discussed later in the text, it is necessary to provide a brief outline of the campaign, its characteristics and the consequences of these to our approach to the problem of identifying successful experiences.

The Adult Literacy Campaign

Public debate of the problems of adults with an inadequate standard of literacy started in 1966, with the publication of an article by Anthony Hirst in *The People*, describing the work of the Cambridge House Literacy Scheme. The significance of this scheme was that adults with literacy problems were offered an opportunity for highly confidential tuition under the supervision of a personal volunteer tutor who provided this service in his or her spare time.

Gradually, a handful of modest schemes, involving relatively small numbers of students, run by both voluntary organisations and local authorities, emerged in various centres throughout the United Kingdom. In most cases, the methods of approach and of tuition were similar to those used by Cambridge House.

Convinced that the problem of adult literacy was widespread, the voluntary organisations, through the British Association of Settlements, formed a pressure group to argue the case for central and local government action to provide a national adult remedial literacy service. The pressure group successfully influenced public opinion by use of the slogan 'A Right to Read', by the publication of testimonies of the daily personal difficulties of adult illiterates and of estimates of two million adult illiterates culled from various tentative surveys, and by evidence of the degree of response to broadcasts on the subject of adult literacy in magazine series such as Thames TV 'Good Afternoon, and BBC 'Woman's Hour'.

When representatives from voluntary and statutory bodies, local and national agencies, citizen volunteers and professional staff, broadcasters, employers, libraries, social and welfare organisations, expressed a willingness to provide help to any adult who came forward with a literacy problem, it was clear that a major national campaign for action had emerged.

Roughly four phases may be identified in the campaign, namely:

1   *Phase I up to mid-1974*, when the main concern was a demand for action – *the activist phase* described above.

2   *Phase II from autumn 1974 to the beginning of 1976 – the period of preparatory organisation*. During this period, the BBC set up their Adult Literacy Project and undertook to produce two television series, 'On the Move' (level I) which started in 1975, and 'Your Move' (level II) which started in 1976, whose purposes were to make contact with potential students and to encourage them to come forward. Supporting radio series to train tutors, 'Teaching Adults to Read', to mobilise potential volunteer tutors and to provide students with reading practice, 'Next Move', were also planned. In addition, all principal broadcasts were to be supported by publications.

A central telephone referral service was planned in London, which potential students or tutors could contact, and similar services were organised in Wales, Scotland and Northern Ireland. Local authority areas appointed referral officers who would receive details of enquiries to the telephone service and would make arrangements for further personal contacts and eventual recruitment of tutors and placement of students.

At the beginning of 1975, central government, through the National Institute of Adult Education, established an Adult Literacy Resource Agency (ALRA) *for one year only*, with powers to administer a grant of £1 million for the financial year 1975–76, to help local authorities and others meet the expected initial increase in demand for adult literacy and to ensure that, by means of a pump-priming operation, adult literacy would be established as an integral part of the adult education service.

In this period, the local authorities trained volunteer tutors, arranged for the accommodation of students and their tutors in centres or in private homes, and *usually* allocated the supervisory tasks connected with literacy to the responsibilities of an existing staff organiser.

3 *Phase III from early 1976 to early 1978 – the period of improving the quality of provision.* The major development was the extension of the life of ALRA until April 1978, with a further £2 million, and a change in the terms of the ALRA grant which enabled ALRA to appoint full-time and part-time staff and, in consultation with the local education authorities, assign them for adult literacy work in LEA areas. The significance of the provision of staff through ALRA's auspices was immense, as the major weaknessess in schemes had been found to be insufficiency of organising staff as such, as trainers of tutors and as supervisory tutors.

4 *Phase IV from early 1978 – the period when the main concern was for the quality of provision which included educational progress beyond literacy.* The life of ALRA ended in April 1978 when it was replaced by an Adult Literacy Unit. The major change was that, from April 1978, the financial support of local schemes was administered as part of the local government education service and any central subvention was now made through the normal procedures of the rate support grant system.

The major characteristics of the literacy campaign

In retrospect we can describe certain features of the adult literacy campaign which together made it a unique historical phenomenon. First, there was the political campaign, organised by a small band of voluntary bodies but enlisting the support of broadcasters, educational bodies and, eventually, Government. This caught the mood of the times in its concern for a deprived minority, and offered an opportunity to follow through the recommendations of the Russell and Alexander reports about the disadvantaged by identifying one such group with apparent clarity. Secondly, there was the planned use of broadcasting as a stimulus to this submerged minority to come forward for help.

Thirdly, there was the contribution of the volunteer tutors. Although some 40 per cent of them had qualifications or experience of some form of teaching, the rest were people whose resource was commonsense experience. Fourthly, there was the institution of ALRA which, in practice, did not confine itself to financial administration but rather encouraged the LEAs to examine their existing service and to establish networks of contacts beyond the bounds of people solely concerned with education. Fifthly, there was the referral service, a unique combination of a central telephone number, widely publicised through the media, with local follow-up services. Sixth, there were the local literacy committees set up by many LEAs, which brought together a wealth of experience from many sources – from welfare organisations, from voluntary bodies and church organisations, from employers, employment services and trade unions and from community organisations – as well as elected members of local education committees and representatives of the education service such as the schools psychological service and careers guidance.

Finally, the campaign was, so far as major educational innovation is concerned, remarkably short: Phase I was hardly more than eight years; the period of preparatory organisation a bare 18 months; the life of ALRA was of a mere three years' duration; the average volunteer tutor had only between eight and 12 hours of training. Thus, the whole emphasis was on action and there simply was not the time for reflection. As one experienced organiser said: 'Things were done very much on the spur of the moment. We were never able to stand back. It all happened piecemeal.'

As a consequence, very little thought was given to the aims of the literacy programmes or to the criteria of success. During Phase II in particular, most training schemes were concerned with methods of teaching the skills of reading and writing, producing reading materials and assessing progress solely in terms of skill acquisition. There was thus a need for a major study of the meaning of success in adult literacy.

Research conducted during the campaign

In January 1975 the Department of Education and Science provided the funds for a research team based on the National Institute of Adult Education, managed by the authors of this book, to study the progress of the literacy campaign.* The terms of reference were, in brief, to study:

(i)   the effectiveness of the campaign in reaching, and holding, the adult sub-literate;

(ii)   the effectiveness of the teaching; and

(iii) the effectiveness of the student's learning as shown in his or her daily life.

Later, in 1976, the National Foundation for Educational Research received an invitation from the DES to investigate methods of diagnostic assessment of progress in literacy skills.

The terms of reference of both these research projects clearly

* cf. Jones H. A. and Charnley A. H. (1978a).

assume an understanding and a definition of the concept of success – a concept which, for reasons we have explained in our brief summary of the campaign, received very little attention from the activists in the field. Consequently, to plug this hole in our knowledge we undertook, as part of the remit of the Department of Adult Education of the University of Leicester, a study of success in adult literacy. This was conducted between early 1975 and early 1978. The period of this research is of some importance as the enquiry needs to be set against a background of events and perceptions prevalent during Phase II and Phase III of the campaign, which imposed certain constraints.

First, an undue emphasis was placed on confidentiality; no student or tutor could be approached unless the organiser of any scheme agreed to the tutor being seen; in turn, no student could be approached unless the tutor agreed and, in addition, the prior consent of the student was obtained. Thus the subjects of the research consisted of that part of the adult illiterate population who came forward and signalled their willingness to receive help *and* who were also confident enough to see a researcher *and* whose tutors were brave enough to allow their student to be seen, and those tutors whose names had been supplied by their organiser. No organiser of any scheme would allow a completely random selection of students from their lists; there was always some student whom they felt should retain complete privacy. Therefore, statistical sampling was not a possible course of action.

Further, as we have explained, the campaign evolved markedly throughout the period of research: there were changes in organisation, training methods, broadcasts, printed materials, tuition circumstances and in the types of students coming forward. Drop-out rates of somewhere around one-third were recorded from lists of those who made the first telephone contact and those who were still in schemes after three months.

Given the pressures on organisers and the difficulties of obtaining returns from tutors in most areas, it was very unusual to be able to obtain any firm figure of the total number of students in actual tuition. This difficulty arose from the voluntary nature of the students' attendance. For example, a student would say that he was on holiday, on shift work or going into hospital for the next three months, and the tutor would continue to register him as being under tuition until it became clear that a decision to break off had been taken. On other occasions the relationship between tutor and student developed more into one of friendship, but nevertheless the tutor still felt that tuition, though intermittent, was still a relevant factor; other tutors, in precisely the same circumstances, would record tuition as having ceased. Thus there was a general problem of getting in touch with tutors and students, and a particular problem of maintaining contact with a particular student over a sufficient period of time to monitor his progress.

To establish any contacts at all, the researcher had to establish a degree of mutual confidence in which both the tutor and the student felt that they wished to help others through the researcher. The researcher had to be perceived as a nonentity, a medium through which the student – and his tutor – explained to the world his experiences and perceptions. In the case of the student he could not, by definition, use the written mode; he had to communicate to the researcher by spoken word and gesture. At the same time, as most students had a limited vocabulary, it was often only by gesture and by tone of voice that the ideas he wished to communicate could be identified.

Furthermore, our preliminary pilot scheme revealed that students viewed overtly-structured questions as a form of testing which reminded them of failure at school and roused in them strong feelings of hostility. Thus, the basic tools of quantitative research could not be utilised. The approach had to be qualitative and imaginative. In the event, our data was gathered from very loosely structured conversations with the students recorded on tape. A similar approach was used with tutors.

Thus, sheer force of circumstances involved us in a qualitative research project. This turned out to be fortunate, for we were able thereby not only to locate commonalities of experience but to point to individual perceptions which themselves both revealed the limitations of generalisations and indicated a further insight into the operation of fundamental modes of human response to perceived environmental challenges.

Because, in the United Kingdom, there seemed to be no evidence of any clear concept of the criteria of success, we had to consider the evaluation of literacy schemes abroad and the criteria of success used in those schemes; in Chapter I, Section 1, we discuss these issues. Next we considered whether the criteria for success were to be found in changes in students' lives in their society and these matters are the subject of Chapter I, Section 2. A further possibility for identifying the criteria of success lay in the linguistic achievements of students; we discuss the potential value of this approach in Chapter I, Section 3.

Chapter I provides the reader with a firm base for making an appreciation of the substantive findings of our research given in Chapters II–X, for as we could not have recourse to some of the traditional objective, or indeed the better known subjective methods, we had to develop new approaches.

1 An approach to evaluation

1 The interpretation of perceptions

Fifty years ago, in *The Bridge of San Luis Rey*, Thornton Wilder created the figure of Brother Juniper, a Franciscan in 18th-century Peru who believed that theology should become an exact science and that 'the world's time had come for proof, tabulated proof' of his faith.

> When a pestilence visited his dear village of Puerto and carried off a large number of peasants, he secretly drew up a diagram of the characteristics of 15 victims and 15 survivors, the statistics of their value *sub specie aeternitatis*. Each soul was rated upon a basis of 10 as regards its goodness, its diligence in religious observation and its importance to its family group. Here is a fragment of that ambitious chart:

	Goodness	Piety	Usefulness
Alfonso G	4	4	10
Nina	2	5	10
Manuel B	10	10	0
Alfonso V	−8	−10	10
Vera N	0	10	10

> The thing was more difficult than he had foreseen. . . . He added up the total for victims and compared it with the total for survivors, to discover that the dead were five times more worth saving. It almost looked as though the pestilence had been directed against the really valuable people. . . . That afternoon Brother Juniper took a walk along the edge of the Pacific. He tore up his findings and threw them into the waves.

Brother Juniper's problem was not the gathering of his data, for they lay all around him, but in their interpretation. His plight is familiar to anyone who has attempted qualitative studies of areas such as literacy: to select a theoretical structure which allows for free and consistent interpretation of the students' experiences. For besides the specific constraints upon research in this area described in the preceding chapter, there are conceptual difficulties that have not been removed by the voluminous literature of educational evaluation.

Much of the relevant literature deals broadly with basic education, including literacy. In this book we are concerned more narrowly with literacy tuition, though we shall later show how arbitrary and unreal such a distinction is. However, the programme in which we worked was a campaign to eradicate adult illiteracy. We were not attempting to evaluate that campaign in numerical, economic or social terms. We were seeking to clarify what might be meant by the eradication of illiteracy, as exemplified in the progress of individual students. How to be sure that 'literacy' had been acquired?

Brother Juniper had three scales of assessment: goodness (or, as we might say, personal development), piety (or public social behaviour) and usefulness (or economic progress). What might be found in these areas in the way of evidence of the successful acquisition of literacy; and what if they revealed as perplexingly contradictory assessments as he found? Who then was to be the assessor, and what was to be regarded as success?

The meaning of literacy

The first difficulty lies in the term 'literacy' itself. It appears to denote a state to which anyone may aspire and which, once attained, will be permanent – like learning to swim or ride a bicycle. Government statements at the beginning of the campaign implied this: illiteracy was something to be eradicated, like slums or malnutrition.

Now the concept of illiteracy is not difficult: it means a total incapacity to interpret written messages. Logic would suggest that it can be eradicated by teaching people to read and write, and that the consequent state, the converse of illiteracy, may properly be called literacy. It is, however, significant that the English language has needed the negative term illiteracy for a very long time – the *Oxford English Dictionary* records it from 1660 – but the positive term literacy was not coined until the end of the 19th century.

There is indeed no direct opposition between literacy and illiteracy, any more than between health and disease. They lie on different planes of abstraction. For example, illiteracy means the inability to interpret any written message, but literacy cannot mean the opposite, the ability to interpret *any* written message. By that definition, who among us could claim literacy?

In fact illiteracy is not an abstract condition but a concrete example of the abstract state of ignorance: it cannot be discerned until some given writing is to be read. Any move away from that form of ignorance is a start on a road which is endless, for the potentialities of language, spoken or written, are limitless. The relationship between progress towards literacy and the nature of language will be reviewed later in this chapter. Suffice it here to say that there is no demarcated state that can be called absolute literacy, with an identifiable threshold. Adult reading and writing always takes place in a context and its efficacy can be gauged only in that context. As the contexts change, the threshold of literacy may change too. Theoretically, therefore, the success of an adult's acquisition of literacy can be judged only in terms of that individual in that situation at that time.

This is the source of a dilemma facing not only researchers but planners and teachers of adult literacy schemes. Problems of diagnosis and measurement of progress have had much attention in training courses and conferences, and in the design of teaching materials. In most subjects, the teacher's strategy will assume that there is a direct line from total ignorance to a foreseeable point that might be called mastery of the subject, will begin with a diagnosis of the starting point on that line, and will include periodic reviews of progress along it. Much of the training for literacy tuition, and the teaching materials prepared for it, has accepted such a strategy without question, despite field experience and the theoretical likelihood that 'mastery' is an inappropriate goal and that each student's progress invites a fresh scale of assessment. Various escape-routes from this dilemma have been tried and it is necessary to look briefly at them.

Reading ages
The first and most common in the United Kingdom is a typically pragmatic one, namely, to import the criteria of children's reading. In the primary schools there is a well-authenticated standard of normal progress in reading from year to year. Attainment according to that standard is expressed as 'reading age' and comparison with chronological age yields a qualitative and objective assessment.

The concept of reading ages has been widely used in adult literacy schemes. Many organisers and tutors have been primary school teachers and carry in their heads approximate measurements of reading age as a quick subjective assessment that they can apply to their adult students. There has also been a general claim that the threshold of competence in adult literacy is roughly a reading age of nine. Among specialists there is a growing recognition that this transfer of criteria from the schools to adult learning is inapplicable and potentially harmful; yet it persists in practice.

Reading ages depend on two parallel progressions of which one, chronological age, is immutable: nothing can stop a child of eight from becoming nine in a year's time. That immutability is an essential part of the measurement, for it offers a prediction of future progress: a normal child's reading age will also rise by one year for each year of chronological age.

Among adults no such prediction can be made. Not only is there an ethical and humane objection to describing a man of 29 as having a reading age of nine, there is also the practical objection that the measurement points nowhere: can he be expected to have attained a reading age of 16 by his thirty-sixth birthday? Or should it be a reading age of 18 by his fifty-eighth?

Furthermore, the type of progress implied in standardised tests for children is largely inappropriate to adults. Tests of readability, for example, which measure difficulty in relation to reading age, depend heavily on the counting of polysyllables, since children start to read with mono-syllables and progress to two- and three-syllable words. Experience with adults shows a quite different order of difficulty. Often they readily grasp polysyllabic nouns, especially social sight words like *telephone* or *tickets* or *post office*, but then have great difficulty with monosyllables whose function is syntactic rather than denotative – prepositions, conjunctions, auxiliary verbs.

The reason for this lies in the general linguistic grasp of the adult as compared with the child and in the character of his spoken language. A man of 29 has the language of his chronological age, whatever his so-called reading age, and his difficulties of reading and writing lie, as we shall see later, much more in the area of his linguistic development than in his stage of mastery of literacy skills. This is clearly seen among born-deaf students whose whole grasp of language is often limited and whose progress towards literacy is constricted accordingly.

In other words, children's reading ages are indices not only of ability to read but of language development. To find some equivalent for adults it would be necessary to evolve an index of language development which could be applied to an individual and then to assess his or her reading and writing against it. Within that thought lies an appealingly simple definition of adult literacy that is sometimes advanced: namely, to establish congruence between the student's speech and his ability to read and write. Certainly that definition gets away from ideas of normative progress and external standards, but the inherent differences of the written and spoken languages make it unworkable.

Basic skills

Another line of escape from the dilemma is to look for an adult equivalent of the normative progress of children. A simple form of this solution is to assert that there are certain basic skills without which further progress in learning is not possible: the threshold of literacy can then be equated with the possession of these skills and anything beyond is called 'post-literacy'. Again the idea has an attractive simplicity. However, we have not so far come across a satisfactory identification of these skills except in terms drawn from children's reading schemes.

Powell (1978) offers a version of this approach with his paradigm of five stages: illiteracy, pre-literacy, basic literacy, career literacy and literacy proper. Pre-literacy (equivalent to grade 4 of formal schooling, or perhaps a reading age of eight to nine) means that some of the basic skills have been learnt but are not yet stable: they may disappear from disuse. In basic literacy (equivalent to grade 7 or 8 of formal schooling) they have become permanent and are there for recall when needed but they still fall short of the demands of adult life. Career literacy implies the ability to apply the basic skills in an advanced way to meet the specialised requirements of adult roles in life. This is an interesting hypothetical structure but the basic skills and their sequence are not specified other than by school grade equivalents.

Some such line of thinking underlies the heavy concentration on phonics that is widely observable in the teaching. Many tutors, including many trained school teachers, have felt that phonic work gave a sound, unequivocal base of skills which could be imparted according to a systematic scheme that would sooner or later sweep up all the problems that a student might have. Once the skills had been mastered the student could apply them as he chose: he had 'learned to read'. The common experience, however, is that adults make but slow progress by these methods and usually find themselves quite unable to make the transfer from practice-with-teacher to independent use in the real world; which is where the next stage of the argument lies.

Competences

However important may be personal development as an educational goal, literacy is a communication skill that implies contact with others: like Brother Juniper we find that goodness alone is not sufficient. Thus a further line of thought about the individual's acquisition of literacy has been to identify certain applied skills or competences that literate adults are seen to display in their lives, and then to measure the student's progress by his command of these competences.

Many different attempts of this kind have been made. Harris (1970) proposed the concept of 'survival literacy' based on a study (in the USA) of the reading requirements of such matters as the application forms for social security, a personal bank loan, Medicare, or a driver's licence. Sticht and his associates (1972, 1975) explored occupational requirements for literacy, and Kedney (1978) has analysed a number of formulations of so-called 'need for literacy' which turn on the same kind of specific competences.

One of the best known and influential of these attempts has been that of Kohl (1974). His schema makes no claim to offer exact measurements but simply enables the teacher to observe broad stages of advancing competence in various identified skills and to assess the degree of assurance with which each is tackled. The stages are described as 'Beginning', 'Not bad', 'With ease' and 'Complex'. The skills at the beginning stage include 'Knowing print', 'Words that connect and words that place', 'Sounds and combinations of sounds' and 'Simple sentences'. The teacher is invited to observe the student's strategy in the application of each skill ('panics', 'evades', 'copes', 'deals'), to assess the confidence shown and to record both the speed and the stamina exhibited by the student in his work.

One virtue of this schema is that it can be used with almost any content, so that progress is being recorded in the student's personal line of advance and not towards some arbitrary external standard. It requires, however, regular operation by the teacher and in practice has been found complicated and slow to apply. It is not a research instrument.

A much more extensive application of the notion of competences is in the Adult Performance Level (APL) programme conducted by the University of Texas. Here the focus is not upon the competent display of skills but upon their result. Three indices of personal success in life are employed: income level, educational level and occupational status. These are associated with three states of functional competence: APL-1 (adults who function with difficulty), with income at or below poverty level, education up to eight years' schooling or less and unemployment or low job status; APL-2 (functional adults), with income more than poverty level but no discretionary income, education of nine to 11 years of schooling and middle-range job status; and APL-3 (proficient adults), with high levels of income, education through high school or beyond and high levels of job status.

The competences associated with these levels of success consist of four sets of basic skills – communication (speaking, listening, reading, writing), number, problem-solving and inter-personal skills. These are assessed in five areas of general knowledge or activity: consumer economics, job-related knowledge, use of community resources, health and knowledge of government and the law. According to an individual's performance in the exercise of these skills, a prediction of his success is made and this is compared with his actual success.

Application of these criteria to a large sample of the US population has yielded some startling generalisations: one person in five functions with difficulty overall, one in three in the area of consumer economics, one in three in computation. As far as literacy is concerned, there is the odd result that 21.7 per cent perform with difficulty in reading but only 16.4 per cent in writing.

Severe criticisms have been advanced of the indices used in the APL study, especially the concentration on material success in income and occupation. But the purpose being to measure performance in a particular culture, the results do demonstrate the relationship between the demands of a given society and command of certain basic skills. Whether this type of study yields evidence upon which an educational strategy can be built is open to question; certainly it gives little help towards the qualitative assessment of the progress of individual students towards the acquisition of literacy in a different cultural milieu.

Functional literacy
Following the emphasis on functionality in the APL programme there has been much discussion of this notion on both sides of the Atlantic. A recent example in this country is an ingenious booklet from the Advisory Panel of the Adult Literacy Resource Agency (ALRA – now the Adult Literacy Unit). It is called *An Approach to Functional Literacy*, borrowing a term coined in the 1960s by UNESCO but giving it a new meaning. It is primarily a manual for tutors but behind it lies a vision of the student functioning, with the aid of his reading and writing, in a world whose reality is determined by his own needs and purposes. Thus the relevant literacy skills are applied to tasks but it is the student who must select or propose the task. A suggested list of tasks includes:

applying to join a club/association
backing a horse
choosing and booking a holiday
claiming Family Income Supplement and other benefits
filling in a pools coupon
looking up a street in an A–Z directory.

The list continues with 27 further suggestions, inviting tutor and student to add more of their own. The component skills of reading and writing are then set out as a repertoire from which selections can be made for the task in hand; and for each task there is an overt result in action (such as a reply to the student's letter) by which he can evaluate his learning for himself.

The booklet is, of course, a teaching aid and not an instrument of evaluation; but it derived from a long process of formative evaluation by the field workers who constitute the advisory panel and is important to the present discussion because of three features that it introduces as a result of that evaluation: first, the identification of functional tasks as a teaching medium; second, the placing on the student the onus of selecting tasks that relate to his perceptions and intentions; and third, the self-assessment built into each task.

The title of the booklet *An Approach to Functional Literacy* recalls the many publications of the 1960s that included that term. The meaning then was different. The phrase 'functional literacy' came into general use following a prestigious world conference on the eradication of illiteracy in 1965 and it was used to denote programmes in under-developed countries where 'development' was the aim. These were usually programmes of technical or vocational training in which the teaching of reading and writing was carried on as an incidental part of the training programme. In this way, it was felt the literacy work would be given relevance and would strongly motivate the population towards participation. The belief was that underdevelopment meant lack of economic growth, that investment in education and training (with literacy as a prime contributor) was the route to quick increases in individual productivity, and that the consequence would be a rising standard of living all round. The Experimental World Literacy Programme (EWLP) was initiated by UNESCO in 1967 to achieve functional literacy (in this sense) in some 20 countries within five years.

In 1976 a study group set up by UNESCO published their report, *The Experimental World Literacy Programme: A Critical Assessment*. It outlines the changes that overtook this simplistic notion of functional literacy in the light of experience:

> In the view of some analysts, however, the strength of the desire to make people literate (which led to EWLP) did not always and necessarily imply its purity. In this view (which is far from universally accepted) the motivation was not to 'do something' but to appear to do something, i.e. to hide a deep determination to maintain the *status quo* behind a mask of superficial change.
>
> (UNESCO, 1976, p. 116)

Two quotations from a thesis by N. Salame are given to illustrate this view:

> It is no coincidence that financial and business circles are showing more and more interest in literacy work. . . . It might provide the dying man with bread, but so as to ensure that others get cake.
>
> (ibid., p. 117)

and:

> There is a risk that functional literacy will supply the economy with individuals tailor-made to fit specific job requirements instead

of enabling each individual to understand, control and dominate progress. (ibid., p. 121)

The *Critical Assessment* is an illuminating exercise in the evaluation of literacy schemes, analysing with honesty and acumen the criteria advanced in connection with some of them – in particular, the problem of identifying success in terms of functionality which the schemes had often posed as their objective. For example, many of the projects dealt with agriculture and not infrequently there was a subsequent increase in the use of fertilisers. Should this then be attributable, the authors ask, to:

(a) newly literate farmers' ability to read, write and do arithmetic; (b) their familiarity with the advantages of fertiliser; (c) their skill in fertiliser use; (d) the creation of a structure for free distribution of fertiliser; or (e) some other project-related (or other) factor?

(UNESCO, 1976, p. 152)

Again, in one country an attempt was made to estimate changes of behaviour as a result of the literacy project and one aspect studied was the use of consumer durables. So a test was applied to a sample of learners and a control group of illiterates about the possession of fountain-pens!

The *Critical Assessment* points out that evaluations of this kind – crude and naïve quantifications – derive from faulty theory. If underdevelopment means inadequate GNP, that was regarded as a quantitative and technical problem. Hence, if literacy projects were to increase GNP, all that was needed was to apply the requisite techniques and the results in productivity would flow. The authors conclude:

A crucial lesson from EWLP seems, then, to be the need to avoid viewing or designing literacy as an overwhelmingly technical solution to problems that are only partly technical.

(UNESCO, 1976, p. 122)

The problems are human, cultural and moral as much as technical or economic. As the authors put it elsewhere, the plain truth was ignored that 'a human being cannot be underdeveloped' in the sense of which these projects implied.

Objectives

The various notions of functionality and competences bring us into the realm of stated objectives. The received truth about evaluation in recent years has been that the objectives of a curriculum must be specified and the outcome can then be measured by the extent to which the objectives have been attained. The question is: what kind of objectives? The production-oriented objectives of some EWLP projects were spectacularly not met, but the consequence was to cast doubt on the objectives and not to condemn the projects out of hand for not meeting them.

The received truth of recent years, however, has tended to favour behavioural objectives as being clearly capable of evaluation. The persuasive work of Mager (1962) and Gagné (1966, 1967), deriving partly from Bloom's taxonomic approach and partly from techniques of programmed learning, had a great influence on early training schemes for adult education tutors in this country: if teachers of craft skills could be trained to specify step by step the behaviours their students were expected to display, clear evaluation – both formative, as the course was in progress, and summative at its conclusion – could be made.

In the evaluation of technical courses, the use of precise instructional objectives has been of much value, not only towards assessing the learning of individual students and the efficacy of course arrangements, but also towards the design and construction of curricula. Where each component skill can be judged against desired performance in actual or simulated work conditions there are clear and objective bench-marks for the evaluation of the teaching and learning. For example, Vilensky and Fraser (1977) list 54 skills to be learnt by students on a hairdressers' course and then compare the timing of each as performed by the trainees with standard timings of professional hairdressing instructors. The efficacy of the training for professional practice is clearly shown by these ratings, both in terms of individual students and in relation to the course as a whole.

Many studies of this kind have been carried out, formally and informally, and many courses have no doubt been improved in consequence. The theory behind them has been well put by Gagné (1967) in a warning against the familiar kind of syllabus that aims at 'covering' the subject:

> It is the defining of objectives that brings an essential clarity into the area of curriculum design . . . the kind of clarification that results by defining content as 'descriptions of the expected capabilities of students'. . . . Once objectives have been defined, there is no step in curriculum design that can legitimately be entitled 'selecting content'. (Gagné, 1967, pp. 21–22)

Evaluating literacy
How applicable is this theory to the design and evaluation of literacy tuition? As we have seen, the emphasis on functionality and the identification of basic skills that the pre-literate adult must acquire look very much like the setting of behavioural objectives. The ALRA booklet on functional literacy sets out its tasks in exactly that form.

On the other hand, the EWLP *Critical Assessment* comes out strongly against a technical approach. It is worth recalling that in non-technical adult education powerful voices have questioned the reliance on behavioural objectives. Elsdon (1975) has pointed out that the areas of adult education in which they could be set are limited and may not be among the most important.

Even in technical courses there has been ground for doubt. Chatfield (1973) examined a technicians' course in Workshop Technology (formerly City and Guilds course 293) to assess each item of the syllabus according to the uses made of it by technicians in a group of engineering factories serving the motor industry. For over half the items the actual use in industry was relatively rare and the potential for use was little greater. There was thus a strong argument for slimming down the syllabus. Yet the technicians interviewed asserted almost unanimously that all items of the syllabus should be retained because together they constituted an important and coherent body of knowledge. In their severely practical view, specific behavioural objectives could define only a part of a total desirable training.

In relation to literacy, there have been a number of studies of what adults actually read and frequency-lists have been prepared. Kedney (1976) has summarised some of these and Barrow (1978) reports another. Newspapers, popular fiction and non-fiction books and magazines and personal correspondence are usually at the head of these frequency lists. But Barrow points out that an index of items of reading regarded as essential has little in common with the frequency lists: dosage instructions, danger/warning signs, emergency procedures, traffic signs and the like then take precedence:

> The filling in of an application form for a driving licence may be a once in a lifetime occurrence, but must be regarded as more critically important than the daily occurrence of reading a newspaper.   (Barrow, 1978, p. 35)

Regarded, one has to ask, by whom? Who shall set the objectives of a basic process like literacy and on what grounds? Might it be that the daily occurrence of reading the newspaper could be more important to the would-be literate than an occasional matter like an application form, for which he would be accustomed to asking for help anyway?

Before attempting to answer this type of question we may look at an entirely different approach to the matter of objectives. Eisner (1969) has pointed out that behavioural objectives belong to 'a predictive model of curriculum development'; and in the discussion of reading ages we saw that the predictive use of such assessments was inapplicable to adults. Eisner goes on to ask, what about those forms of education in which the outcome cannot be predicted as behaviour? How would you specify the behavioural objectives of studying, say, *Paradise Lost*, or the Crusades, or wood-carving? In answer, he advances the notion of 'expressive objectives' which are unpredictable in behaviour, are 'evocative rather than prescriptive' and which may be expected to result from what he calls 'educational encounters':

> The expressive objective is intended to serve as a theme around which skills and understandings learned earlier can be brought to bear, but through which those skills and understandings can be expended, elaborated and made idiosyncratic. With an expressive objective what is desired is not homogeneity of response among students but diversity. (Eisner, 1969, p. 16)

For the teacher, adult literacy tuition will usually appear to be predictive: the student will eventually 'be able to read'. There is then the temptation for the teacher to import instrumental objectives, as in the stages of a formal reading scheme. If we ask what it is that the adult will learn to read, for what purpose, with what depth of understanding, with what result, we see that there is no linear progress here, such as could be assessed by an advancing series of objective tests. Each piece of reading or writing is a domain of its own, defined by the student's purpose and these purposes derive from his status as an autonomous adult, exercising will and judgement within the context of his own life and aspirations. Only a child can learn to read; an adult learns to read something and to some end.

Champion (1975) has offered 'intentions' as a preferable alternative to the customary term 'needs' as a description of what we should be looking and responding to in our transactions with students. This distinction is sharply applicable to the literacy student. We have shown elsewhere (Jones and Charnley, 1978a and 1978b) how progress in literacy is bound up with the growth of the student's confidence – not simply confidence in his ability to learn, although that is part of it, but rather confidence in the assertion of his intentions and in the contemplation of the self in making the assertion. Such confidence is preliminary to any progress in reading and writing skills. It begins with the student's discovery of his tutor as an adult who will accept his identity, taking notice of him and his intentions and treating them with seriousness. Where tutor and student have common interests, or where the student's special knowledge is picked up by the tutor and used as part of their shared work, momentum quickens and horizons widen. The student's immediate objective becomes subsumed into a longer and unforeseen development.

This is very close to what Eisner calls an educational encounter.

The literacy student needs to find 'a theme around which skills and understandings learned earlier can be brought to bear but . . . expanded, elaborated and made idiosyncratic'. The ALRA manual shows an understanding of this. It offers specific instructional objectives as a proximate means but allows the student's intention, revealed in his choice of tasks, to give the reality, the drive and the perception of the ends. The major objectives therefore lie in Eisner's expressive domain; there is no predicting where the encounter might lead if it has the right quality of relationship and is not trammelled by instrumental objectives imported by the teacher.

Acceptance of this approach to evaluation also helps to avoid the temptation for planners and initiators of adult literacy programmes to specify behavioural objectives or functionalisms prescribed by cultural and social norms and not by the student's own choice. The temptation can exist in advanced countries (as the cultural specificity of the APL criteria shows) and underdeveloped countries alike. The dangers of using literacy schemes as a form of social engineering, under the guise of 'development', have been underlined by the EWLP *Critical Assessment*. For the preservation of a free and equitable society (which must be one of the political components of the decision to embark on a literacy programme) the autonomy of the individual, however disadvantaged, must be respected, and evaluation of educational programmes such as a literacy project must always start from that point.

This is not to say that social or even economic ends are inadmissible, but only that they shall be there as practicable options open to the student's choice. At the World Conference on Adult Education in Tokyo in 1972 the director-general of UNESCO, warning against 'a much too narrow economic sense' in which functional literacy had commonly been seen, went on to say:

> The idea of functional purpose ought to be kept in education . . . [to] emphasise the relationship which exists between education and society's needs and between education and the motivations and aspirations of the individual which . . . have been too long disregarded. (UNESCO, 1972)

(There is of course also a relationship between society's needs and the motivations and aspirations of the individual: this will be explored in the next section.)

Here we simply conclude that the balancing act invited by the director-general is not easy to sustain. Brother Juniper's problem with Alfonso V, with minus marks for goodness and religious observance but a full 10 for usefulness, and with Manuel B (10 for goodness, 10 for piety, 0 for usefulness) illustrates the difficulty. To evaluate gains in individual development, social competence and economic functionality invites three different types of objective and three different scales of assessment, each giving partial and potentially incompatible results.

The way through, as so often in the education of adults, is to allow the students to lead. In the interpretation of their perceptions as recorded by research, the evaluation of success in the acquisition of literacy must begin with the objectives perceived and formulated by the students, and not with externally imposed standards and purposes. For it is in the perspective of individual lives and intentions that the three kinds of objective come into a common focus that permits assessment of the rich range of outcomes, successful or not, from the educational encounters of the project.

2 The social location of the students

If our initial hypothesis about the evaluation of success in adult literacy is, then, that it must rest on the student's intentions, it follows that we must examine the pressures upon those intentions. This takes us into the realms of motivation and the social location of the students.

Hypothesis-formation is not new in this area. Very little hard evidence has been assembled about students in the UK literacy schemes, but that has not prevented a deal of hypothetical formulation, or what might unkindly be called myth-making, especially at the outset. We have already noted, as a constraint upon research, the common expectation that the literacy student would be afflicted with a crippling sense of shame about his condition and that he must therefore be assured of absolute confidentiality, even secrecy, over his entry into tuition. Similarly, there has been a common assumption that illiteracy bore, and was felt by the student to bear, public stigma. There was an assumption that those needing tuition were 'illiterate', in the sense of being quite unable to read and write. And, as will be shown in more detail later, there was a tacit, perhaps even subconscious, assumption that the potential student would be severely disadvantaged, with low income, low occupational status and low level of participation in community or social affairs.

Hence one of the aims in the interpretation of the research data will be to note indicators that confirm or refute these assumptions. What evidence already exists about these matters? The main sources are the ALRA annual reports, the research by the National Institute of Adult Education (NIAE) (Jones and Charnley 1978a) and a number of local studies such as those by Risman (1975), the Liverpool Project (1976) and Kedney (1976, 1978).

First, on the issue of shame. There is no evidence about this in most of the sources which were concerned with demographic and sociological data rather than feelings and attitudes. The NIAE research, however, did establish that, whilst many students showed reserve about their condition and had to acquire confidence in their self-perception before they could make progress in tuition, the supposedly crippling effect of these feelings was not generally visible. Where the student's reception into a scheme was welcoming and reassuring, and especially where contact with a peer-group was made at an early stage, the inhibitions and anxieties began to fall away.

Secondly, about stigma. There can be little doubt that the whole literacy campaign, especially the broadcasts, brought the question of adult illiteracy into the open and focused the public mind upon it in a quite unprecedented way. The enrolment of thousands of volunteer tutors also gave to that section of the population first-hand evidence of the existence and the effects of adult sub-literacy. The result of this, as revealed in the NIAE researchers' interviews with tutors, was often to provoke their anger at evident and unsuspected defects of the educational system. Almost never was it to stigmatise the student.

How far the public mind generally has been affected it is impossible to say. Indeed, there is no certainty that the supposed stigma of illiteracy existed widely at all. It was one of the working hunches of the organisers. But Holmes (1976) has argued that the feeling of stigma may itself have been fostered by the literacy campaign.

> It seems clear that some students do feel ashamed . . . but it is very easy for middle-class values to assume 'the shame of illiteracy'.
>
> (Holmes, 1976, p. 159)

In some circumstances the very success of embarking on tuition may increase the fear of being defined as inadequate and the consequent feeling of stigma:

> . . . if the student becomes socially mobile and begins to fear the stigma of illiteracy as seen by potential new reference groups. . . . Is the price that will have to be paid for the extensive publicity operation . . . the growth of feelings of shame as the whole operation becomes a kind of crusade? (ibid., p. 159)

Thirdly, there is the question of level of knowledge. The EWLP *Critical Assessment* says:

> It was generally assumed in EWLP that the beginning learners were fully illiterate. This was far from always the case.
>
> (UNESCO, 1976, p. 174)

Both the assumption and the finding are even more true of the UK project. Something like one-third of the students who came forward were 'beginners'; that is to say, their very limited ability in reading extended little beyond the recognition of certain social sight-words – somewhere between Powell's pre-literacy and basic literacy stages. The remaining two-thirds were distributed more or less evenly over a range of ability that reached high competence in reading and writing but difficulty in spelling. To speak of the students as 'illiterates' is therefore quite inaccurate. Indeed some of those interviewed hotly repudiated the label as being equivalent to half-wit: they were not, they said, like that. Accordingly, we have come to use the term 'sub-literate' for the full range of people at whom the project was aimed.

Fourthly, the social and occupational status of the students did not accord with the prior assumptions. Typical of these is the comment in a report on 88 students in Liverpool:

> It has long been obvious that the bulk of adult illiterates come from socially disadvantaged groups. It is also equally clear that as long as they remain illiterate they will be unable to find employment in any but unskilled roles.   (Liverpool Project, 1976, p. 5)

Yet the figures for this selection of 88 students show that 20 per cent were already in semi-skilled and 12 per cent in skilled occupations at enrolment. Risman (1975) lists the occupations of 82 students in the scheme at Reading and concludes:

> It would be dangerous to assume that our students are seriously economically disadvantaged. Few in fact, in so far as they are in full and regular employment, would appear to be any more economically disadvantaged than their reading counterparts in the working-class community.   (Risman, 1975, p. 145)

The NIAE research team found that many of the volunteer tutors were surprised at the degrees of skill and responsibility required for the jobs held by their students, and at the special and extensive knowledge they often revealed of their avocations and leisure activities.

None of this is to be taken as meaning that adult sub-literates are never in disadvantaged or deprived circumstances but simply that, on the evidence available, there appears to be no necessary connection between lack of literacy skills and low social and occupational status.

The assumption of such a connection lies behind a number of studies, such as the concept of 'survival literacy' of Harris (1970) and to some extent of the APL criteria; and also behind some prescriptions for teaching exercises which concentrate on the reading involved in application forms for benefits of various kinds, citizen's rights and the like. That these are needed by some students would be undeniable; but that they are needed by the bulk of the present students is not the lesson of the evidence so far.

The student population

It is therefore pertinent to enquire into the relationship of these students to the norms of our society: why these students and not others?

We must remember that those undergoing regular tuition in literacy, and therefore within the cohort studied by researches like the present one, are only a selection from those originally coming forward for help: some 30 per cent disappeared within three months of making their first contact. Moreover, those coming forward during the first two years of the campaign (at most 100,000) form only about 5 per cent of the two million claimed as the target at the outset. This latter figure has never been authenticated nor its scope defined. But if the population at risk is taken to be that embraced by the *range of ability-levels displayed by the actual students* (including the competent readers and writers with chronic spelling problems) then it may well be much larger than two million.

In other words, we are looking at a small surviving group, out of an originally small minority, out of a quite large minority of the adult population. That large minority are not self-selected: they are victims of the education system, of genetic dispositions, of ill-health, or of other conditions. But the subsequent minorities, those who came forward and those who persisted, *are* self-selected. The factors affecting their selection form a much more complex, and potentially more informative, range of concepts than those usually comprised under the heading of motivation.

Marginality

The sociological concept of marginality immediately suggests itself in connection with this selection process. Are not these sub-literates indeed 'marginal men'? One recalls the ethical justification given for the EWLP literacy schemes:

> to enable them to throw off one of the strongest chains binding them to a second-class citizenship. (UNESCO, 1976, p. 115)

Second-class citizenship is not the same as severe deprivation, but it does imply separation from the centre of society: a marginal status.

This status of the adult sub-literate has nothing in common with the marginality, or liminality, identified by social anthropologists (for the priest, the medicine-man, the tribal chief-elect) as being charged with magical power. Nor is it like the prestigious voluntary marginality (or disengagement) of some intellectuals and inhabitants of counter-cultures where transformations of consciousness are being sought. Initially at least, it is an involuntary state deriving from exclusion by a literate society from the tramlines of social mobility or job advancement. So it stands at a remove from what Berger calls the 'middle ground' of society, the taken-for-granted in everyday life.

Berger's view of marginality, however, is related to the possibility of change. Those who become separated from the taken-for-granted values of society and move into marginal positions are more open to change because the accustomed symbols by which they chart their relation to others have been removed or abandoned. Moreover, the 'recipe knowledge' by which they have made judgements and decisions no longer seems applicable. But in a pluralist society such shifts are constantly being made and perceptions of centrality and marginality may vary considerably between groups and in the same group over time. The Third World sharply illustrates the point:

> In countries where 80 to 90 per cent of the population is rural, illiterate, often property-less and without access to basic social services, while 10 to 20 per cent is urban, educated in largely alien schools, owns or manages the means of production and consumes according to a Western-inspired standard – who is marginal? . . . Who is to be integrated into what society? On what terms?
>
> (UNESCO, 1976, p. 119)

In *Margins of the Mind* Musgrove (1977) has studied seven groups of people who are in marginal positions. Some, like his Hare Krishna converts, are there from choice; others, like his blind persons and his inmates of a Cheshire home for severely disabled, are involuntarily there. Two responses are identified: 'passing', that is, behaving as though still part of society's centre even when involuntary marginality is imposed, as upon those who have gone blind; and 'coming out', or openly embracing the marginal status as a means of liberating the true self. The most instructive in this connection were his group of homosexuals who had, after varying lengths of time spent in 'passing' or concealing their condition, made the deliberate choice to 'come out'.

The similarity of language between this 'coming out' and the adult student's 'coming forward' suggests some common element in the experience. But there is a radical difference. Whilst phenomenologists, following Schutz, have accepted the notion of 'multiple realities' and the subjectivities of people's inhabiting of them, there is generally an assumption of a single centre to which these various sub-universes are marginal. That position would not explain the Chinese box of minorities to whom the literacy project was addressed or the process of self-selection noted above. The large minority of sub-literates in the population – the two million or more – are marginal to the values of the main society in matters of education and qualification; but there is no evidence of a widespread desire for change. The small minority of them – the 5 per cent or so – coming forward for tuition are at a point of change: they are now marginal to their former 'centre' in the sub-literate population. They may be said to represent what the UNESCO team, noting a similar process of self-selection in the Third World literacy projects, calls 'an élite of the impoverished'. The steps by which this 'coming forward' is achieved are not dissimilar from those described by Musgrove for some of his groups: the pressure of family or 'significant others', the slow recognition of the possibility of change, the feeling – once the step had been taken – that the 'true self' had been found.

This view of the process also helps to cast light on the early losses (often inaccurately called 'drop-outs'). An appreciable number who telephone the referral points are never heard from again; a further number never take up the offer of tuition after an initial interview. The common view is that the system has somehow failed them, but the theory of transformation from marginality suggests that this may not always be the reason. The marginal state has its advantages: it may be easier to go on 'passing' as one of a large group of sub-literates than to 'come out' with an acknowledgement of former marginality. The first step towards the centre may bring the nature of the change vividly to light and cause withdrawal as from a brink.

This is speculation, for non-participants were not accessible to the research. But the point accords with a number of UNESCO reports which found 'change-resistance' in many of the populations approached with literacy projects (UNESCO, 1965a, 1974); with studies such as that of Goldberg (1951) in the US Army ('in most civilian situations the illiterate does not see the benefit in learning to read and write'); and with the experience in Illinois, reported by Cook (1977), where illiterate recipients of relief would forfeit their money if they did not attend an educational programme and of 270,000 on relief only 7,000 joined the programme ('the undereducated did not want to learn'). Some confirmation of the hypothetical sequence outlined above may then be seen in the interview-data recorded, especially where respondents were recapturing the memory of their earlier lives.

Adaptation and survival
One other concept now comes into the perspective, that of adaptation for survival. The change of life sought after coming forward is a

process of chosen adaptation to a new habitat. The awareness of failure, and of being defined by others as a failure, is no doubt near the surface of consciousness of the whole sub-literate population, even when it is overtly denied: for example, concern for one's children's education is not an exclusive prerogative of the literate. But counterbalancing that is an undoubted awareness of success in other directions, as the volunteer tutors frequently discovered among their students. Much of the symbolic world and the recipe knowledge of working-class cultures, as Hoggart reminded us years ago, does not demand literacy.

When, however, one of this sub-literate population comes forward for tuition in literacy, he is deliberately shedding the protective colouring of his old habitat and seeking adaptation to a new one. Moreover, the new habitat is one which he will perceive only dimly and the process of acquiring this fresh adaptation demands not only changes of protective colouring on his part, but a sharpened perception of the world he is adapting to. It is not fanciful to describe this process in terms of survival; but it is not survival in Harris's sense, of simply finding one's way through jungles of forms and regulations (for which one can easily find help). It is the acquisition of a new identity – or perhaps the assertion of a 'true self' – among scales of values that have to be learnt. Hence we said previously that access to a daily newspaper may well be more important than applying for a driving licence.

The guide is the teacher, who will be expected to embody the mores of the new world and yet to be sufficiently understanding of the old to make effective communication. The delicacy and the paramount importance of the teacher-student relationship is clear enough.

This theoretical model suggests a set of hypotheses about the social location of the adult literacy student and his intentions. He is one of a self-selected minority of a minority, seeking to identify with values long rejected, moving from a newly-acknowledged marginality towards a centre as yet unknown. He is thus one of an élite, but not an élite ambitious for power or place. He may be seeking acceptance and security but in the assurance of his own self-perception rather than, or together with, the perceptions of others: he wants to be 'I' and not simply 'me'. Accordingly, his intentions are backed by a very heavy investment of his self-regard, which will leave him as vulnerable as any species in an unfamiliar habitat.

3 The demands of speech and writing

The student approaches his new habitat through language. He has to extend his linguistic competence from the directness of the oral language to the indirect symbolism of writing. A great deal of literacy tuition proceeds as though this is a simple process of mechanical transfer from sound to letter and back, with occasional digressions to lament the 'illogicality' of English spelling. To understand, however, what the new reader faces we need to understand the basic differences between speech and writing, between the oral and the written languages. For the fact that in English we have a fixed orthography and certain conventions of punctuation and syntax appears to give to the language a uniformity that is in truth spurious.

Simple examples will illustrate the point:

1   A teacher of English in a Devon school was once observed tearing her hair in frustration because, for the then O level English syllabus, she was required to teach the grammatical cases of pronouns in sentences such as 'She gave it me'. But what the pupils *said* in their own language was, 'Er give it Oi', with the standard case-forms reversed and a different form of the past tense of the verb.

2   A local radio station in the North of England decided to assist the adult literacy scheme in the area by broadcasting a series of local folk tales, with a printed text to accompany them so that literacy students could follow the written form while listening (after the style of the BBC *Next Move* radio series). The tales were, of course, in dialect; they were correctly broadcast so, and proved very popular with listeners. But what of the printed version? How can you represent such a statement as ''Oo were off down t'bank' (= She was off down the bank, or hill) in a written form that will not grossly conflict either with what the student is learning from printed materials elsewhere, or with what he is actually hearing?

3   Later in the book we transcribe excerpts from the tape-recordings of interviews with students. We have attempted to reproduce as faithfully as possible their actual speech. But there will be many instances where it is obvious that the conventions of written English are quite inadequate for this purpose and where the meaning emerges only when the reader begins to reconstruct the spoken form in his head.

This is the kind of problem met every day by teachers of literacy to adults, though training courses appear to pay little attention to coping with it. For the researcher, however, what is important is to gain insight into the range and nature of the linguistic difficulties the adult sub-literate has to surmount in order to survive in the new habitat to which he aspires. Two sources may be drawn upon: contemporary linguistic theory and comparative experience from other countries. The former helps to identify relevant concepts about the nature of language and its social situation. The latter offers, as so often, examples of acute practical problems and solutions attempted.

The nature of language

Any language comprises three elements: sound, meaning and syntax. Our first contact with language is through the sounds. The number of sounds that the human speech organs can make is limited – although no language in fact makes use of all of them. Yet because of the semantic and syntactical structures we have developed an infinite number of meanings can be expressed with these few sounds, for we have evolved beyond the point where one sound has one meaning – as a bird might have one call for fear, another for food, another for mating.

The development of writing, however, particularly at the stage of general literacy reached by Western countries, has changed the way in which we think of language. We all know that there is a greater range of sounds used by English speakers than the 26 letters of the alphabet, though we may not realise how many more: we can joke about words ending in '-ough' but few of us recognise the difference between the aspirated 'p' of 'put' and the relatively unaspirated 'p' in 'spite'. Yet we have no vocabulary in which to speak of the sounds. When we attempt to do so we use the names of the letters – the written symbols. When we fail to catch the sound of a word, such as an unfamiliar name, we ask for it to be spelt – that is, put into its written form.

The sound structure of a language is immensely rich. Each language has a repertory of distinguishable sound-patterns or groups, traditionally called phonemes, which are the bricks out of which spoken messages are constructed. In most languages the phonemes do not wholly coincide with the written letters; in English the coincidence is very imperfect and often seems arbitrary. The 'c' and 'k' of 'cook', the 'k' and 'ck' of kick', the 'q' of 'queue' and the 'K' of 'Kew' belong to a single traditional phoneme. In a purely oral language, their identity would be apparent. In ours it is masked by the visual memory of the written letters. Conversely, there are sounds for which English has no written equivalent. In the dialect phrase 'down t'bank' the abbreviated form of the definite article is pronounced by a glottal stop (written(ʔ) in phonetic script): it has nothing to do with the 't' phoneme. Similarly, the intermediate or neutralised vowel (written (ə) in phonetic script) is variously spelt 'a' (normal), 'e' (letter), 'i' (permissible), 'o' (potato) and 'u' (awful); but it has no letter of its own.

A language is not, however, simply an accumulation of sounds of the vowel/consonant type: that is what the halting literation of the reading-beginner sounds like. Each language has sound-patterns of pitch, stress, tone, length of sound and so on. In English an upturn of pitch at the end of a statement generally indicates a question: in writing we have to represent this with '?' But not all questions are spoken so. The question 'What did you say?' can be uttered with a variety of stresses and intonations that can convey a simple request, or puzzlement, or accusation, or threat; and these cannot be adequately represented in writing. A hearer hears them; the reader has to recreate them.

It will be apparent now that, for most of us, the spoken language is an unfamiliar and unrealised world. We operate the conventions without understanding them because we lack labels to identify them. In so far as we conceptualise our language at all we do so through the letters and words of the written language.

The second component of language is meaning. We have seen how in speech varieties of meaning can be expressed that the written language cannot convey. 'Writing', said Bacon, 'maketh an exact man.' This is only partly true. Certainly writing can attain a greater precision of statement, a precision defensible on legal or logical grounds; but speech is a richer, more flexible, more evocative, more affecting mode of communication. This is partly because the speaker has the range of tones, stresses, speech tunes and pace at his command; partly because he also has a repertoire of non-verbal signals or para-language – pauses, gestures, facial expressions, sniffs, sighs, tears, laughter; and partly because of the differing syntactical structures of the spoken and written languages.

Syntax and grammar have formed an area of great controversy among linguisticians. In relation to literacy, however, the most informative distinction is that between the deep structure and the surface structure of a language. Central to the deep structure and its syntactical rules is the sentence, which can be regarded as a noun-phrase plus a verb-phrase (or, as we used to say, a subject plus a predicate). The surface derives from the deep structure by the operation of complex series of rules. For our purpose, all we need to note is that the spoken language has more evidence of surface structure than the written, which is closer to the deep structure.

What this means in practice is that we write in complete sentences: subject, or noun-phrase, plus predicate, or verb-phrase. We may learn to cultivate various forms of composite and complex sentences, to acquire stylistic techniques of balance and rhythm, to practise subtleties of apposition and punctuation. We may learn to write in different 'tones of voice' – formal, scientific, hortatory, familiar, colloquial. But the conventions are pretty strict and departures from them are effective only when the basic standards are known and taken for granted.

In speech, on the other hand, we imply but do not assiduously form complete sentences. We offer a subject without formulating a predicate. We embark on sentences and alter the structure half-way through. We resort to locutions like 'you know' and 'you see' because most of the time we can be reasonably sure that the hearer *does* know or see: he is there, reacting visibly to our words, and providing what communication theory calls immediate feedback. In any case, our spoken messages are quite often not intended to carry information, but are small talk, or what Stuart Chase called 'social noise'; that is, they have emotive or affective, but very little cognitive, content. Finally, we all spend much more time speaking and listening than writing or reading.

The result of all this is that the conventions of the spoken language are looser and more variable, and that individuality is more possible. Indeed, speech is one of the major features of the personality: a person's voice, his manner of speaking, the forms of words he customarily uses, the pace, pitch and tone of his speech, his employment of gestures and non-verbal signals, all contribute to the demonstration of his identity, and they do so every day in every interaction with other people. Moreover, Chomsky draws a distinction between competence and performance in language: we know a good deal more of the language than we use. Hence we have, especially in speech, reserves upon which we can draw if we wish to extend the range of discourse.

By the time, therefore, that he has reached adult life every speaker will have established his ideolect, a personal style of more or less richness and subtlety, developed to cope with the customary situations of his life and the pursuit of his intentions. This was what was meant earlier when we spoke of the linguistic development of a man of 29, contrasting it with a supposed reading age of nine. The less he has had recourse to reading and writing, the greater may well be his resourcefulness in the spoken language, particularly in receiving and interpreting other people's oral messages. To assume linguistic impoverishment because syntactical patterns do not conform to the conventions of sophisticated writing is to misunderstand the basic nature of language and perhaps to risk the error that one of the UNESCO reports so sharply reproves:

> Have not illiterates survived for centuries in milieux (such as the Andean *altiplano* and the African Sahel) which would have proved lethally hostile for precisely those urban literates who judge illiterates insufficiently 'integrated into the milieu'?
>
> (UNESCO, 1976, p. 119)

Dialects

Dialects exist in speech but not, for modern English, in writing. Dialect is an indicator of origin, of a group belonged to. Often when we wish to indicate approval of someone, we embrace them linguistically: 'I like him, he speaks my language.' Dialects which were once defined by geographical boundaries have come to acquire social boundaries: there are social or class dialects.

The written language is in certain respects like another dialect.

It has a formality of structure that speech usually lacks, it has 'correct' forms that are not recognisable in speech, and it has a very limited range of conventions for the communication of the emotive component of utterances (so that the gushing letter-writer is driven to underlining). The student who reads and writes with fluency but has difficulty with spelling and punctuation is one who has entered only imperfectly into the written dialect: he has not mastered its conventions and is relying on the surface structure of his spoken language for guidance which, in the nature of things, it cannot give. Not all 'bad' spellers are worried about their state: their writing is rarely unintelligible. Before 1700, very few would have worried, because orthography was not fixed anyway and there was rarely any resultant ambiguity. What brings forward the few who seek help with their spelling is the feeling that they are failing to reach the *social* norms of the written dialect, not its linguistic requirements: they feel excluded from the tribe.

Once again the Third World literacy projects throw a sharp light on the matter. In some countries there has had to be a political decision which to choose as the official language from among a number of dialects that have no written form. In such situations, theory suggests that it is preferable to make people literate in their home language first and then develop their literacy into the official language. The home language is a bridge towards literacy in the official language. But in practice many students of such schemes are impatient of the bridge: they want to get on into literacy in the official language. Baucom (1978) mentions one small literacy scheme with classes in three home languages and one official language; there was a total of 14 students in the home language classes and 565 in the official language classes.

Sometimes a so-called union language is created for official purposes. This is an invented written language that can be read by speakers of all dialects in the country. Written English, thanks to its historical development in the last three centuries, has become such a union language. Its form varies little over the whole world and is equally intelligible to literate speakers of widely ranging and sometimes mutually incomprehensible dialects.

No one so far has suggested that sub-literate adults in the United Kingdom should first be taught reading in their own dialect as a bridge towards literacy in standard written English (though some special schemes such as Initial Teaching Alphabet have an element of this in their composition); and it would be foolish to attempt it. But that should not obscure the special features of the written language that make it a much less accessible habitat than may be thought for the sub-literate adult with a greater or less degree of confident achievement in the spoken language.

31

4 Summary

At the centre of this research is the adult sub-literate student. (We tend to refer to 'him' because in the early stages of the campaign four-fifths of the students were men.) He is a member of an élite minority, and he is there because as an autonomous adult he has formed intentions that lead him there. The world he aspires to enter – what we have called his new habitat – is linguistic and the adaptation called for is determined by the nature of the written language; but the process of his self-selection for that adaptation is social and the basis of the motivation lies in his perception of the self-in-society. Although concepts of shame and stigma may not be uppermost in his motivation, the change from margin to centre that he purposes is one that leaves his self-image vulnerable. His persistence in approaching his new habitat will depend on his reception there – the educational encounters with his teachers and others – and the measure of his success must start with his intentions, or expressive objectives, and work within his perceptions of the adaptations he is required to make, rather than through the application of formal and external standards.

II The design of the research

Certain postulates were made in the early stages of our research, which influenced both the design of the research and many of the detailed procedures which we finally adopted. First, we accepted that literacy – the mastery of the medium of the written language – could not be separated from linguistics, the study of language in all its manifestations. In Potter's (1966) description:

> Linguistics stands in its right place in the Dewey Decimal Classification between sociology and natural science because it is a social activity on the one hand and a scientific system on the other. It was an outstanding achievement of nineteenth-century philologists . . . that they succeeded in establishing the autonomy of their science as an independent discipline in its own right. Now, by a kind of paradox, twentieth-century linguists find themselves more closely associated than ever before with researchers in other fields, not only in history, geography, practical criticism, philosophy and psychology, but also in mathematics and statistics, physics and electronics, and, above all, in anthropology and the social sciences. (Potter, 1966, p. 175)

And, as Potter points out and re-stresses later in the same book, linguistics is a *social activity* as well as a scientific system. The rub of the matter is that the adult student seeking instruction in literacy rightly regards it as a skill which will lead to other accomplishments. Thus, we assumed that the criteria for literacy achievement would comprehend more than increments in the skills.

Secondly, we stipulated that people needed to be literate. We regard the process of becoming literate as part of the process of becoming educated, that is, the nurture of personal growth. Growth is an end in itself, a fulfilment at each stage of living; it is personal in

33

the sense that, if a man adjusts to his reading, not only does he respond to the content of the written words but he brings his own individual consciousness to the symbols. Viewed in this way, the aims of literacy are ultimately those of education. One part of being an educated man is the ability to be literate and, in so far as it is necessary to be educated, so is it necessary to be literate. We know that some are better educated than others; we accept as a moral value that people should reach the limits of their potential in educational terms and so, to be consistent, we must argue for literacy. But it follows logically that there are various levels of literacy abilities and that, perhaps, adequacy at any level of achievement depends on skills, on societal requirements or individual psychological needs.

Thus, we thought of achievement in literacy as a record of progressive growth and dismissed the notion of a static terminal which, once reached, qualified a person to be described as literate. It became clear that measures of an adult's achievement depended on individual starting lines, and that our investigation should be designed to encompass these degrees of particularity.

Thirdly, early in the investigation we discovered that, in practice, literacy projects cater for people with a wide range of literacy problems.

For example, the problem was posed when some students said:

Before I could about write my name and address, but now I'm learning all the time. You see, I want to learn now. I've got so much that I want to learn more.

Reading has always been difficult, but I could read words like 'and', 'was' or 'cycle'. I can now write a word, look at it, and say, 'Yes, that's right.'

I could read reasonably well. It was the writing, the spelling, words like 'chicken' and 'lorry'.

I can't really explain. I went on a course where I had to read but I felt it because my mind went blank. Yet I know I can read. I've no trouble with filling in forms. I'm afraid to write it down. . . .

Interviewer's question:
If I had come into this room and asked you to write something, could you have done this?

Student's reply:
I think I could have done so but I would have asked you, 'Do you mind turning round?' I don't know what it is, it's just there.

Or in a letter from one tutor:

Hence the odd phenomenon of people with *managerial* literacy applying for help, *because they need reassurance about their standards.*

Consequently our approach had to be based on a theoretical structure which allowed us to describe a student's experience as a *whole*, including his reactions to his perceived environment. For this reason, we utilised an adaptation of the methodology developed by the comparative ethologists.

The ethological approach

The ornithologist, David Snow, describes the problem of explaining the behaviour of birds in tropical forests as:

collecting as many facts as one can, and by inference, by comparison between species, and by using what others have found in related fields, one builds up hypotheses that are consistent with biological theory, so far as it is understood. (Snow, 1976, p. xii)

The processes are, therefore, to observe, to infer, to refer, to relate, to hypothesise, to re-observe and so on, or, following Tinbergen (1963), to start with inductive descriptions of observable phenomena and then make a *comprehensive* approach to several problems thus identified, giving equal attention to each of them and their integration, using throughout a *scientific method* of study (the biological method). The ethologist accepts that 'description is never, can never be, random; it is, in fact, highly selective, and selection is made with reference to the problems, hypotheses and methods the investigator has in mind'.

The first step, the initial observation, is of quite a different order to that applied in orthodox empirical investigations; for example, when choosing the data to be samples (and observed), statistical, quantitative sampling methods rely 'on a *preconceived* theoretical framework'.

In the ethological approach, the criteria for the choice of observable data are based on general experience and the researcher's analysis of the level of cohesiveness and integration of the theoretical approach. As Snow (1976) remarks:

Without theories and hypotheses one only has a jumble of facts. But one can over-indulge in facile explanations; if one's theory is wrong, one can go badly astray. . . . The facts, if accurately observed and described, will stand for all time; the theory can *at best be only provisional.*

Consequently there is an open-minded collection of data through observation, there is a process of interpretation when significant behaviour is selected and, through a process of consideration of the consistency of the elements of the gathered data, re-interpretation and generalisation follow.

Thus it seems that the ethological approach may describe accurately the efforts of *all* people, whether in advantaged or disadvantaged groups, by placing their actions within the context of their attempt to adapt in order to survive. But, patently, human beings differ from animals in their subjective image of themselves, others and their concept of God, life-force or of the 'ought'. Because this is so, the ethological method as applied to animals becomes an analogical system when applied to human beings, and within it there needs to be the phenomenological concept of, for example, allowing the student to define reality in terms of his own subjectivity.

Consequently the methodology adopted in this study is to record the subjective impressions of students and tutors and to view their concepts of success within the framework of a struggle to adapt to survive. By using phenomenological *data* and by following the *procedural* steps of the ethological methodology, it is possible to understand that, in an adult illiterate's concept of what may be necessary for his adaptation and survival, 'success' may be very different from that envisaged by a tutor operating in a different universe of discourse, faced with different conditions for survival.

The ethological approach is the key to understanding the educational behaviour of all disadvantaged groups; that is, all groups with restricted codes of discourse and communication.

The preliminary stages of the investigation

A thorough examination of the criteria of success in adult literacy in the appropriate literature, published in the United Kingdom and overseas, led to the listing of 25 statements which could be judged as possible indicators of success. After the completion of a survey of tutors' characteristics in one local authority area, a questionnaire was devised, asking tutors to use their own judgement, regardless of any experience of students' aims, of the importance of each criterion of success (see Appendix A, Section A). However, from the comments accompanying the 149 returns, from four local authority areas, it was doubtful if any answers were given that were entirely free of considerations of the needs of, or experience with, a particular student. Although the results of the questionnaire had to be interpreted as being of limited validity, they remained useful as part of the *total* evidence. Part B of the questionnaire asked tutors to suggest further criteria of success. These are listed in Appendix B and were grouped into 12 major categories as preliminary criteria.

Summary of preliminary criteria of success

In summary, the 12 major categories of criteria for success were:

1 the building up of confidence
2 financial or occupational survival
3 reading for pleasure
4 reading and writing as an integral skill within the field of adult education
5 student acceptance of responsibility for the process of achievement
6 development of personal psychological harmony
7 the development of easier familial relationships
8 improved societal relationships
9 non-vocational interest development
10 linking literacy skills to other knowledge areas and personal experience
11 development of oral skills
12 linking literacy skills to personal long-term education.

As a further check, just in case our original list of 25 phrases had been too directive, we compared these results with the returns of an additional group of 26 tutors who replied to a simple general question: 'What level of achievement would you count as a success for your student?' included in an independent enquiry (see Appendix C for replies).

On the basis of all this evidence, by a process of statistical ranking we identified five categories of achievement, and we were able to place these categories in descending order of importance as follows:

1 Affective personal achievements
2 Cognitive achievements
3 Enactive achievements
4 Socio-economic achievements
5 Affective social achievements.

A further problem was investigated, namely: did the tutors' opinions of the priority of the criteria of achievement change through time? From the answers to our questionnaire (Appendix A, Section B) we found that the phrase 'regular attendance at classes' was regarded as being the most important initial signal of achievement during the first few weeks, but 'general improvement in confidence and bearing' was considered to be the prime achievement at the end of the course. However, the most important result at this stage of our enquiry was to show that most respondents had no experience of taking any student beyond a period of six months. On the basis of this evidence, therefore, it could be neither affirmed nor denied that the length of the course would play a major part in the establishment of tutors' aims.

Consequently a further instrument of research was constructed, consisting of an analysis of three case studies conducted over a period of 10 weeks by three teachers taking the advanced education course at the Cambridge Institute of Education. In two cases there was a definite movement in the tutor's scale of objectives, whilst in the third there was apparently little change. Through the use of the 25-phrase section of our tutor questionnaire (Appendix A), we constructed histograms of the attitudes of each of these three tutors to the criteria of success at the beginning and end of their 10-week periods of tuition. We were thereby able to quantify the change in the order of priority of each tutor's objectives as listed in the 25-phrase questionnaire, and the degree of change in attitude to each criterion. From this analysis it appeared that it took at least 10 weeks for tutors to establish the fundamental motives for their students registering for tuition, but after a period of some six months tutors were able, with confidence, to state the criteria by which they judged the success of their students.

Therefore we decided to record our conversations with tutors and students during the first six months of 1976 and, following *a lapse of 12 months*, to repeat the interviews, in a shortened form and with some additional questions, in the first six months of 1977. Although this dealt with the problem of change in the tutors' attitudes to the criteria of success, it did, however, mean that there was a risk of many of the students having ceased tuition and not being available for a second interview.

The sample

The following evidence, presented in a way to protect both tutors and students from being identified, is based on the tape-recordings of conversations with students and tutors derived from:
(a) the profiles of 68 students as described by 49 tutors, and
(b) interviews with 35 out of the 68 students.
The remaining 33 students were not interviewed because over half had ceased to have tuition between the initial contact with the tutor and

the date of arranging to see the student. Of the rest of the students not interviewed, some did not wish to be seen, some were on holiday and others had suspended their lessons for the time being.

Of the 68 students under consideration:

(a) 44 were male
(b) 24 were female
(c) their total average age was 32 years 9 months
(d) the average age of the men was 31 years 7 months
(e) the average age of the women was 34 years 8 months
(f) the range of age was from 16 years to 56 years 6 months (with an exceptional case of one in the early sixties).

The sample was taken from two types of organisations which provided facilities for students, namely:

(a) the local authority – 32 students
(b) the voluntary organisation – 36 students.

The local authority organisation provided tuition in:

(a) a tutor's home – 4 students
(b) an adult education centre – 25 students
(c) a library – 3 students.

The voluntary organisation provided tuition in:

(a) a tutor's home
(b) a room in a community centre provided by the local authority
(c) a mixture of (a) and (b) above.

Nearly all the students made their first contact with the voluntary organisation in the community centre, but thereafter about 30 of them continued their tuition in their tutor's home. However, of these 30, some six to eight also met their tutors in the community centre occasionally.

There were various types of tuition schemes:

(a) *The local authority*

The local authority offered alternative modes of tuition:

— home tuition solely with a particular tutor;
— tuition solely with a particular tutor in a local authority-maintained building;
— tuition with an individual tutor under the supervision of a tutor organiser, other students and tutors being present; and
  class tuition, usually five to eight students with one class tutor.

In the event, however, the local authority arrangements for tuition, by place of tuition, consisted of:

(i) *An adult education centre* (25 students)

Here, during a period of two hours, each student would have individual help from a volunteer tutor. Pairs of volunteer tutors and their students were distributed around the room under the supervision of a tutor-organiser who taught particular students, organised and often supplied resources.

(ii)   *A library* (three students)
These students formed part of a group of four (the fourth student did not attend during the period of the research) meeting in the local library. Each student had an individual tutor, and a tutor-supervisor exercised overall control.

(iii)   *Meetings at home* (four students)
Each student visited the home of his/her tutor for tuition and was taught solely by his/her particular tutor.

(b)   *The voluntary organisation*
The voluntary organisation concentrated solely on one-to-one tuition so a student would receive tuition from his/her own tutor, whether the tuition took place at the tutor's home or in a part of a classroom in the community centre. Students in this scheme who met at the centre did not meet each other for coffee or for any other reason during their tuition period. Usually the tutor met the student in the entrance hall and together they selected a private corner of the classroom for tuition; at the end of the session, tutor and student left the building together.

Attendance patterns

As the adult education centre scheme had been the longest established, many students had attended for periods of three, four and even five years. The average period of attendance was, at the date of interview, respectively:
(a)   23 months at the education centre,
(b)   10 months in the local authority tutors' home provision, and
(c)   9 months in the voluntary-organised scheme where students usually met in the tutor's home.

The analysis of quotations

In the following chapters quotations are selected from lengthy, largely unstructured conversations with students and tutors to derive criteria of success and to establish an understanding of the meaning of those criteria. In this chapter the procedures for analysing these tape-recordings are described in some detail, for the interpretation of such material is always difficult and the inevitable element of subjectivity (which is present also by design in the data) has to be made clear.

In particular, it will be shown that, whereas the criteria based on the answers to the questionnaires to tutors were in rank order:

(a) affective personal achievements
(b) cognitive achievements
(c) enactive achievements
(d) socio-economic achievements
(e) affective social achievements,

the perceived criteria that emerged from the tape-recorded evidence were, in order:

(a) affective personal achievements
(b) affective social achievements
(c) socio-economic achievements
(d) cognitive achievements
(e) enactive achievements.

Moreover, within each of those five major categories certain sub-criteria were identified and located in rank order. Similarly, in the next chapter, students' perceptions of their educational experience and social background are deduced from quoted statements. Here the same problem can be seen, in that some statements of perception are selected as being of more importance than others.

When the fieldwork was completed, there were many tape-recordings; those of the tutors were linguistically more sophisticated than those of their students, whose statements were usually couched in a simple, halting, imprecise code.

Therefore it seemed crucial to the investigation to ensure that the recorded evidence should produce patterns of perceptions *endogenous* to the data on the tapes. As a cautious scientific procedure, it was decided that the exogenous hypotheses described in previous chapters *should be disregarded*. If the evidence of the tapes contradicted or augmented the previous descriptive studies of perceptions, then logically a contradiction would be viewed as being the equivalent to a nullified hypothesis, and should an additional piece of evidence emerge it would have to be considered.

To ensure the procedural independence of the selections of recorded data, the following steps were taken, steps 1 and 2 being carried out immediately, or as soon as possible, after the interview, with step 3 *et seq.* being carried out before the chapters with the quotations were written:

Step 1

Each tape was transcribed by a sole interviewer. No transcriptions were made by a secretary, who would not know the exact circumstances under which the recording was made.

Step 2

The written transcription was read and the circumstances under which it was taken were noted. For example, the presence of a spouse and/or tutor and/or student was noted. Some tutors would not be interviewed unless their husbands were present; where his presence affected the course of the interview, this was noted.

Step 3

Each written transcript was read again and checked against a play-through of the recording to refresh the memory of the tone in which the comments were made and of the gesticulations which accompanied the statements and, where necessary, these were noted on the transcript.

Step 4

Transcripts of the conversations with tutors and students during the first and second interviews were re-read to locate corroborative statements by either tutor or student or repetitions of statements made during any of the individual interviews.

Step 5

Each written transcript of the tape-recording was then re-read, and where a statement was relevant to educational or social background, or to any form of achievement or success, this was copied on to a separate slip of paper.

Step 6

The total pile of these slips of paper was then placed in heaps by subject matter. *The subject matter was entirely determined by the nature of the quotations on each slip of paper. The only imposed classification* of the tapes was that specified in Step 5 above.

Step 7

Each heap was then placed in a *row* by reference to the subject matter of each heap: e.g. a heap with statements about using a literacy skill in shopping would be placed in the same *row* as a heap concerned with other uses of literacy skills.

Step 8

Each *row* was then read through again for a possible classification and, by continuous rearrangement of associative heaps, six major *rows* emerged, which could be classified as follows:
— perceptions of educational and social background
— affective personal relationship achievements
— cognitive achievements
— enactive achievements
— socio-economic achievements
— affective social achievements.

There were some rows left over, containing no more than two or three slips. These slips were re-read to ensure that the problem was that the quotations were difficult to place within the six categories listed above rather than that further classifications or re-classifications of the rows were required. In the event, it was discovered that these awkward slips indicated an individual's aberration of perception from the majority of the rest of the quotations. Consequently they were added to the six rows and included in the following chapters as examples of a highly individualised, unique perception.

Step 9

Quotations in each row were re-read and placed once more in individual heaps on the basis that the six major groups of row titles were indeed correct.

Step 10

The heaps within each row were placed in order according to the number of slips in each heap. Thus, when a quotation appeared several times in *nearly* the same words, that heap was regarded as expressing a single perception. But even though the heaps were ordered by frequency of quotation, when a quotation appeared only twice, or even once, or two heaps had the *same* number of quotations, the recording itself was listened to again to see if the vocal emphasis and the place of the quotation in the context of the total conversation implied that the quotation represented a perception of major importance to the speaker, or the perception expressed was worthy of greater emphasis because of our own knowledge of further corroborative evidence. If either were the case, the perception was given a greater weighting than its numerical frequency position originally suggested, and that heap was moved upwards towards the head of the row.

Step 11

Then the chapters were written, using the quotation slips but in the order of the replies given by the tutors to the questionnaire from which the five major criteria were originally derived.

Step 12

As each chapter was written, the slips of quotations as placed on the table in rows and heaps determined the structure of that chapter and within each chapter 'groupings' of perceptions emerged which were summarised at the end of each chapter.

Step 13

Then each chapter dealing with the five major criteria was read again, to establish the relative importance of the sub-criteria within each chapter, and the effects of the total evidence given in each chapter. It then became clear that the taped evidence produced a different order of importance and ranking of criteria from that evinced from the replies to the questionnaire sent to tutors. It is this final ordering of the perceptions of students and tutors that is advanced as a conclusion.

Step 14

Quantitative descriptions

When a heap was more than about two-thirds up a *row*, the term *most* is used as the adjective in the following chapters. When the heap was more than about two-thirds down the row, the adjective used is *few*. Quotation heaps between approximately half-way and two-thirds up the row were allocated the adjective *many* whilst those half to two-thirds down were called *some*. *Very few* in that context describes quoted perceptions at the end of the row. All adjectives take into account tonal evidence and the use of other communicative modes.

The above description of the procedure adopted contains two major methodological issues which need further discussion. These are:

(a) the justification for the statement in (10) above 'or the perception expressed was worthy of greater emphasis because of our own knowledge of further corroborative evidence', and

(b) that the use in (14) above of the adjectives 'most' and 'few' or variations of such adjectives in the following chapters has the sufficient degree of exactitude necessary for the formulation of conclusive generalisations.

The use of corroborative evidence

The explanation of this facet of the investigative approach lies in the ethological or, in more strictly stated terms, the comparative ethological approach which has permeated the methodology of this thesis. When an ornithologist and ethologist studies a particular bird within a particular species, that bird's behaviour is carefully observed and described. It is then interpreted both in the context of various ecological, social and behavioural influences and also in relation to the observed behaviour of other members of that species. The ornithologist compares and contrasts one particular member of a species with other members of that species and with other species displaying similar behavioural patterns.

A similar process has been applied in the case of the study of the perceptions of the adults, both students and tutors, whose statements are quoted in the following chapters. Thus, in deciding that 'the perception expressed was worthy of greater emphasis because of knowledge of further corroborative evidence' we had in mind, in general, three years of work on the NIAE research project and, in particular, 26 visits to local authorities to discuss the problems of adults involved in literacy schemes. It should be stated that, in our view, this general background knowledge was an essential component in the ordering of the 'heaps' of quotations within the rows, and of the rows, and in understanding the *significance* of sometimes isolated snippets of evidence.

The element of subjectivity is acknowledged, but the claim is that the researcher is not simply a camera with an open shutter. Where he is himself engaged in the field of study – as is common in educational research – his professional experience will inform his interpretation of data just as does the ethologist's ecological knowledge. This is the justification for applying the term 'corroborative' to such knowledge. Corroborative knowledge is, in particular, useful when dealing with students whose skill in articulating their thoughts is very variable. One is forced to interpret whilst at the same time accepting the subjectivity of such interpretations.

The device of such adjectives as 'most' and 'few'

There were alternative ways of proceeding. First, it would have been possible to count the number of quotes in each heap and to have simply given the number in the text; one could have said that 20 students said that and 16 said this and to have thereby implied a simple weighting of five to four. But to have done this would have been to mislead the reader, because no quotation was outside a conversational context, the environment in which the interview took place and the emphatic tonal quality of the response or even the explicit accompanying gesture. It has already been noted in previous chapters that there was a variety of students, of varied levels of articulative skill, within the relatively small total number of people available for interview.

To say that 'most' students, for example, perceived 'confidence' as being an achievement of prime importance in their scale of success is to interpret the following type of conversation:

Student: Well, I feel better – you know – you know – I feel better. Yes, I feel – well, you know – easy – yes, easy – in myself, you know. Do you see what I mean?

It was the grin and the general context and a statement towards the end of the interview that:

Well, I'm getting on very slowly with my reading – very slowly – but it's helping me in a sort of way, in myself which led to a translation of the student's perception as being:

I am gaining in confidence first and foremost.

If 'most' students expressed this perception in this way, one can only truthfully write 'most', even though an exactitude, spurious though it may be, might offer a sense of well-being to the quantitative mind. 'Most' and 'few' and such adjectives are all that can be offered at this stage of the investigations into the perceptions of achievement among adults concerned in literacy schemes. The crux of any scientific venture is the awareness that someone else may add to the contribution of this grain of sand to our knowledge of adults with problems in literacy; such future endeavour will be that much better based if the present methodological problem is clearly stated.

Secondly, it would have been possible to index each quotation by means of a formula incorporating vocal qualities, emphasis in context and frequency of statement or frequency of persons making similar statements. To have done so would have led to the objections already rehearsed in the previous paragraph. In fact, the presentation of the evidence would have been less open to critical inspection by the reader because of a greater number of judgements being involved in any index system.

Thirdly, it could be argued that nothing so complex in quantitative terms was required; rather, a simple statement that so many students or tutors said this or that. But, because of the largely free conversational technique with tutors or because of the language register of students, no two people said *exactly* the same thing and it seemed highly dangerous to apply additive arithmetical procedures to non-identical items. Particularly in the conversations with students, too structured a questioning technique would have resulted in surprising responses. As an example of the ethological approach in action and the use of what Rosemary Jellis calls 'a natural experiment':

Interviewer: Have you used the library?
Student: What do you mean?
Interviewer: A public library.
Student: You mean the town library? No!

So far, the answer to the question, fairly structured, is 'No!' So the interviewer could reasonably have gone on to ask the next structured question, but the student's expression was such as to indicate that he was not quite satisfied with the conversation to date, and the interviewer waited. After a pause:

Student: I've borrowed books, though!
Interviewer: Where from?

Student: Well, Mr. X has arranged a room in the council to have books for us.

The student was quite right; a room had been set aside in the council building where the librarian ran a rather less formal sub-library especially for such adults, so the answer is 'Yes!' because the student had borrowed books from the library.

The problem used as an example is a simple one. Of course, it may be argued that by careful pilot questionnaires and so on, questions can be arranged to require only one specific type of reply. But there are two further problems, as shown by the pilot studies already mentioned: first, it was normally possible only to use simple questionnaires with highly verbal or literate people (tutors) and, secondly, the nature of the perceptions of adult illiterates was not known sufficiently well enough to devise a comprehensive questionnaire which could be applied even by verbal interview.

There remains one further comment that may assist the reader in his understanding of the following chapters, and this concerns the use of a concept of survival in a particular way.

Survival – the underlying theme

The way in which the perceptions of students and tutors were ascertained and ordered has been described above, and some indication of the final major ranking of criteria has been given. Similarly, before discussing the quotations in detail, it seems appropriate to indicate the belief that all the evidence points to an underlying and pervasive desire to survive. The term 'survival' in this thesis does not mean such processes as obtaining enough food to live – that is not, at present, a difficulty in the United Kingdom – nor does it mean the passing on of genetic characteristics of a species or a race of mankind. It means, rather, that in modern industrial societies human beings have a problem of survival which stems from their unique ability to choose to accept themselves as they are and to continue to live. To survive, human beings need to be within certain limits of tolerable self-acknowledgement or of self-image. At one extreme, the intolerable may become so great that survival is utterly rejected; though suicide is an awesome sin to those versed in the tenets of Christianity, such action may provide the only possible relief from unbearable anguish. At the other extreme are those who live in a cloud of unctuous self-regard and self-satisfaction, and whose self-image is one of undiluted admiration. The hypothesis throughout this text is that 'most' people exist somewhere within these limits. The adult with a knowledge of his deficiency in reading or writing or, that is, an adult who thinks he is illiterate (for, as we have seen, few in the sample were totally illiterate) seeks to ameliorate his self-view of his worthiness.

The hypothesis has therefore been propounded that the adult student who came forward in this sample was, in fact, appealing to his tutor for two reasons: for technical aid in a particular skill and for help to re-burnish his self-image to enable him to cope with the stress of ordinary day-to-day life in an extremely complex and sophisticated industrial society.

It is worth reiterating that this hypothesis was *ignored* when selecting the quotations, ordering the quotations or assessing the quotations in the 'rows' or 'heaps'. It was only as the following chapters were written that the idea of 'survival' as defined in this chapter emerged, and the notion seemed to provide an appropriate thematic key to understanding the activities of students whose literacy skills ranged from those who could read and write fairly well to those who experienced great difficulty. If this idea of 'survival' as defined is acceptable, then there may well be the hint of a basis for the understanding of the problems of people who, for one reason or another, lack the ability to share a characteristic which is displayed by the majority of their contemporaries.

The following chapters illustrate this theme in so far as it concerns the adult who sees himself as being one of the few who bear the burden of having a literacy problem.

III Students' perceptions of their educational experience and social background

Educational experiences

Without exception, every student left school as soon as legally possible, well aware of his or her inability to read or write or spell correctly.

> I think I had problems with it all . . . by the time I was 15, with the whole lot; a right mess. I had trouble and a hard job to write where I lived, even my name, for a long time. And when I went to work, I had to do that, to prove to everybody that I could read and write when I could not!

> I did not find difficulty in reading – only in spelling. I do not know what happened in the other subjects – History, Science or Mathematics. I was pretty good at Mathematics, Algebra – you see. I would not consider myself a brilliant student; I'm not a scholar, or anything like that! But let me put it this way: in Mathematics, I finished top of the class, in English, I finished up last. I left the day I could because I hated school.

But very few students shared this extreme view: most recollections of their schools, as a whole, were mixtures of pleasures and dislikes, and the greater the emphasis placed by one school on purely literacy skill performance, the deeper the discontent recalled.

> In no way were they impressed with the way I could spell and this was a stigma in this type of school because from 11 years of age you were taught – you *are* going to be a secretary! So how could I be a secretary when you could not spell?

49

But where the school was more concerned with education a student recalled that:

> I can remember starting off school not really bothering, you know. So long as there was a game of football going – thinking – this is it! This went right through until the last year of school; then a schoolmaster there gave me a bit of a talking to and pushed me a bit – I could read and I quite enjoyed school but I think I could have been pushed.

However, most students realised that they had a literacy problem long before their last year at school; 65 out of the 68 students had progressed from primary to secondary schools, some students had been to quite a few schools within each sector but the norm was to attend one primary school and one secondary school. One extreme case was that of a student who:

1 started at an infants' school
2 went to a junior school – also in hospital for a period
3 was evacuated to East Anglia – another junior school for three months
4 returned to the junior school, referred to in (2)
5 was given eyesight tests and sent to school for partially sighted
6 was sent to another school for the partially sighted
7 was returned to the school for partially sighted mentioned in (5) at the age of 13 years and remained there to the age of 15 years.

His experience was encapsulated as follows:

> It was the school I was at for 18 months that I really enjoyed – it was a special school, but it was a very small school. You knew everybody and that was it, you seemed to get on with the teachers there. Most of the teachers seemed to muck in with the children. It's difficult to explain it – *it was more of a home than a school!*

A similar case was that of a student who said:

> I think the difficulty was that I was never at one school long enough to settle down. Each time I moved to a different system of teaching – if you don't settle into that system you have had it. Between five and seven years I went to two infants' schools. Between seven and 10 years I went to three junior schools, where I took the first half of the 11-plus examination but left before I took the second half.
>
> At 11 I went to a secondary school, then half-way through the second year I moved again. I missed two months, but attended for the end of term and the beginning of the next term of my third secondary school. Then I missed school again until half-way

through the third term. Again I moved to another secondary school where I stayed until I was 15.

There are those who consider that adult literacy is largely a problem of non-attendance at school for one reason or another. To some extent this is true, and the above cases illustrate this point, but a closer inspection of the students' perceptions and accounts of their youth suggest that non-attendance at school was the sign of a disorganised family life. One student had sought in his school the stability of a home, another had suffered from the eccentricities of her mother.

Furthermore, the problem of their reading and writing performance usually appears in their earliest school days and, more often than not, their secondary school experience is merely an account of how the problem was exacerbated. For example, one student said:

> I was frightened of school from the very first day. I remember the Headmistress dragging me away from my mother. I remember so well; I can see her face now and particularly a pair of blue sandals that she wore. I was five, but it is so outstanding in my memory! Being dragged away from my mother and just not liking school. Well, as I got older, I thought – well, it's obviously because I'm a dunce and can't learn.

Another student could vividly recall her youth and when asked if she was getting along quite well at her infants' school, replied:

> All I can remember is that one day my mother complained about the fact that I wasn't making the progress that I should do – this was to the teacher and not to me. I had not worried about it at all in fact. The amount of English we were doing was a very small amount anyhow. That was at the infants' school, I think. It was at the junior school that I realised that my friends were getting on with it and I was not seeming too good at it. Because of the fact that I found it hard I lost interest and then when I went to a secondary modern I found it a bit more necessary to try and do something with it: but it never developed. There was always a corner that I could not get over. I would get so far with – personally, talking about schools now I think I went to the wrong school. I should have been at a special school – to go into a normal school was mistaken.

But some students did not recall any problems emerging at primary school level. One tutor, speaking about her student, said:

> According to him, he remembers working at a primary school and learning to read up to the age of eight or nine. He remembers what he calls lessons. He thought – he felt – that he was all right

at primary school and it was a *shock to the family* when, *as he describes it*, someone came to the door and his parents signed a form and he went to an ESN school.

Nevertheless, the bulk of the evidence from the students' perceptions suggests that they were aware of their problem before they were eight or nine years old. The emergence and development of the problem was described by one student as follows:

When I was eight I had sunstroke and I was away for 12 months. I can remember that I tried to read then but I could not. The teacher said I should not worry because I could go in the garden and that is where I spent my time – and that was when I was 10 or 11. At 11, I moved away from x to s – (about 20 miles away in the same local authority area) – they did nothing at all. They put the remainder of you in a lower class; they put them all together – but you came to woodwork or metalwork it was very interesting because you could make all these things. You had no paperwork at all; the *others* made plans of it. It would be very useful now to make plans. I could make anything; I did not do no plan at all. You did a lot of gardening – all in school time. I ought to have learnt but I could not *grasp* it because *I had bypassed the important part before I was nine*.

He had attended two schools, one primary and one secondary, and he should have been able to read before his illness.

The experiences of the students of their secondary schools seems to depend on the student's generation. Those who completed their school before 1939 seem to have attended senior departments of the same school and to have jogged along at the tail end of their class. A student who left school in 1929 simply did not differentiate between secondary and primary school, but her perception was:

In my generation, I can understand; I can see my teacher now, 'No, not you, Jane. On to the next one!' Because I spent a lot of time at home, no one took the trouble to teach me.

The post-war secondary modern schools created by the Butler Act of 1944 tried to raise the standards of the most disadvantaged children by creating special classes, or remedial classes. Some adults experienced this system:

My brother could not read, he was in the Q class in our school, which was very low; it was the dunce's class. He joined (the Services), he now has GCE O and A levels in English, Mathematics and History – actually just passed A level English! (Left school some 10 years ago.)

Another student described such a class:

> I was in the special class, because there was a class on its own –
> about a dozen of us. We went into other lessons but when it comes
> to lessons – we went into woodwork, gym, arithmetic, science,
> history . . . the backward children went into another school (prob-
> ably class), like at eleven o'clock in the morning or two o'clock
> in the afternoon. ('Did you think of yourself as a backward child?')
> Well, yes, I did. (Pause) Well, no, I would not say I was backward
> but I was forward in other things!

On the other hand, some students recalled their 'special' or 'back-
ward' class as having helped them. For example, the following evidence
given by one student says much for the sensitivity of his teachers in
the special class:

> I spent two years of my schooling spent in a class of people who
> were then called backward. Two years of it, right! I thought this
> was very good, I picked up, which gave me a lot more interest in
> life, *not just reading*, and through those two years and then after
> that, because there was only one teacher, you see! We were flung
> out into the main stream and that is when . . . (long pause). Some
> subjects I got along all right with; other subjects like reading, I
> was just at the *bottom of the class all the time*. There is no way that
> you could do things like exams and things like that. *We were very
> fortunate* because it was a smallish class and three of us, that were
> down, used to have exam papers *read to us so that one could answer
> them*. It would still have been better for us to go to a school where
> we could all have been taught together instead of being chucked
> in with a lot who were better. I mean I did just as well in science
> and subjects in which they did not do so well. The only 'first' I
> ever got was in science but I came third in technical drawing.

Most schools persevered with considerable obstinacy to help their
pupils, but quite often the transition from a special class to a normal
class was traumatic. The same student quoted above continued:

> Basically what happened was that I was so bad – even compared
> to the three that came up with me – that I used to have two
> periods a week, when I went to the third year, going back to my
> old class doing reading there. Then, the fourth year, they decided
> that we were going to be flung out into the big wide world. At
> that period, they decided to try and drum the alphabet into us.
> Which even – well, now I can do; but then, it was all in bits. They

decided to teach us that for one period a week and that was in the
fourth year. Again, if I had had a special (school), if I had been
in a school for it, it would not have happened – the backwards
and forwards business.

A more recent system was to provide special remedial lessons in
literacy skills. Speaking of the early 1970 period a tutor described his
experience as:

> I retired – they had been advertising for somebody to take remedial
> work with a third year – I rang up and told them I fancied the
> job and he said, 'Come in! Start today!' I went in to see them a
> few days before to talk this over. I was given the reading ages of
> 22 pupils (13 to 14 years), five Italians, one Pole, one Ukrainian,
> several Pakistanis, some native English. Of the English children
> the best performer had a reading age of 9.3 years, the worst a
> reading age of 5.3 years. I found this class had never had an exam
> – appalling – nobody was interested! They had been advertising
> for somebody to take this class and nobody had applied – no
> applications!

More recently, the remedial services have made even greater efforts
to raise standards and more effort has been concentrated in the primary
sector, but whatever the educational organisation *there will always* be
poor readers or writers. Schools are concerned with the education of
the whole person – and whilst no school teacher would lightly take
the pressure from a pupil to read, there are sometimes overwhelming
social or psychological reasons for relaxing the concentration on literacy
skills. One such example is contained in the evidence given by a student:

> I started school at five; well, I could not do nothing at all – then
> I had to go into hospital, I did not get much school. I started back
> at school when I was coming up to six years old. When I was six,
> my writing just picked up. A teacher used to come in from another
> class when he used to have free time. He would help me. He used
> to help me a lot. Every teacher with a free lesson used to help me.
> When I was nine years old, the writing and the spelling got better
> and better all the time. And when I was 11 I started at the X–Y
> School and I started learning my lessons better, *just keeping my
> nose clean, not bothering anybody else in lesson time* and everybody
> used to – the headmaster (I was in the fifth year) would say, 'Tom,
> I have got some parcels coming in a lorry. Do you think you
> could go down and deliver them in the classroom?' – The head-
> master only put me on that because it used to help me with my

reading. 'We have a job for you to help you read (titles of books). Any mistakes or anything you can't read, go to Mrs — and she will help you.'

By remarkable patience and individual attention the school kept him out of court whilst he was there, but social pressures and personal psychological ineptitudes in the end triumphed and within a year of leaving he had begun what appears to be a criminal career. This is an extreme case, but the evidence of students did suggest that often an unspoken pact was reached between pupil and teacher, the principal clause being, 'You leave me alone and I'll let you get on teaching the other 30 or so pupils.' As one student described it:

So we sort of – I was a bit of a maniac really. I was one of those boys that – not really liked school – I used to like boxing. – Well, I think I must have been lazy – I was out playing football all the time – but I don't blame *them* really because it's up to the individual really. – I used to go to school regularly. My mother and father used to *make* me go to school. ('Did you enjoy school?') I think so, as far as I can remember it.

Another student described how the contract worked ('Did you enjoy school?'):

No, I did not (sharply said) – I did not enjoy it, I used to be behind the class, because some of the words I cannot understand, you see. I cannot sound them. We did not have much extra teaching because we went up with the class. We got behind. Sports, woodwork, gardening were all right. I was top once in gardening. I won three or four prizes at school for gardening. I have not missed (being away from) school at all.

To be charitable, it has to be added that the school kept him sane and encouraged his out-of-class interests. Several students described school as reasonably happy experiences and many identified lessons or subjects which they liked. In all cases, the less the demands made on their literacy skills, the better they liked it. Thus, practical subjects such as woodwork and games figure high in their scales of preference, or subjects capable of being presented and understood diagrammatically or visually such as geography or history were favoured. The men mentioned sport and practical subjects, though one student disliked metalwork because he continually had to draw plans. The women chose domestic crafts, needlework, cookery and dancing as their most enjoyable subjects.

The most likeable teachers were usually in charge of the most likeable subjects; nevertheless, certain teachers with charisma were mentioned regardless of subject. Some students expressed clearly their prejudices:

> I never got on well with female teachers. Mr. X was very disciplining, I did more for him than I had ever done.

In general one suspects that though most students said they hated school, the following view was not particularly rare:

> I did not have very happy school years, I hated it. I did not like work, I wanted to go back to school – but I knew I could not!

Indeed, nearly all the students were not referring simply to school, the teachers or the curriculum. Rather they were describing the deeper relations of youth, their relations with their peers in school, their parents' view of the school and their school progress, their perception of themselves as failures.

> When all the children were put together – some got it, some did not – I did not!

These are perceptions of failure: first, by those whose sensitivity centres on literacy and, secondly, by those who found school a thwarting experience even though they are effectively literate for most purposes. In both cases the sense of failure may originate from over-expectation on the parents' part or from social conditions outside the control of the school. Nevertheless the students' perceptions of that social background are recalled largely in the indirect terms of their accounts of their schools and much of our knowledge of their social background comes from the students' accounts of their parents' relationships with the schools, or their own relationship with other children in the schools.

Perceptions of social background

In nearly every case the homes of the students' parents lacked books; there were magazines perhaps, but certainly not anything approaching domestic libraries. Yet the brothers and sisters of students often had jobs requiring literate abilities and one wonders how they managed. The most plausible explanation is that they were taught to read in their primary schools (there are, indeed, some exceptional primary schools who rarely produce non-readers) and that they continued to improve throughout their secondary and higher education.

Most students' parents tended to leave formal education to the schools; some parents visited the schools when something attracted their notice. Such an event was graphically described by one student who, on discovering her son's inadequacies, visited the school:

> One day (her son, aged about eight) left me a note – it was at the back of the clock – it was *two* words that I could understand, and that was the number! I was appalled by it! I went to school, I could not even get past the secretary and no one wanted to know! (Eventually she saw the teachers.) They said, 'Oh! I can assure you, Mrs. X, it comes, it comes.' Putting it straight up, that's a load of * * * * * *, *it doesn't come*. It only comes to the very few. It doesn't come to people unless they are taught.

More typical is the experience of Jill:

> I don't think my mother pushed me; we are not a shoving lot. We like gentle persuasion.

Conditions have not changed; Jill describes her present relationships with her child's school:

> I know from my own child – we have been round there and talked until we are blue in the face but we don't get anywhere. I don't go any more, I send my husband and he is getting somewhere, at last, because we are not happy about her – I have a pen friend and I deliberately asked her about her children (in Scotland) and she has the *same* problems with her!

Asked 'What did your parents say about you making no progress at school?', a student replied:

> My mother went after them, and wanted to know the reason why and what not. But she got no satisfaction.

Thus the students' homes ranged from the caring to the totally indifferent; one student described her home background in the phrase:

> Mother? If you can call her that!

The professional/managerial home background was the exception as were, though not quite so much, the social misfit families. Normally, the family in which the students were raised consisted of a tolerant father and a slightly worried mother who together provided, on the whole, a happy background. Most parents could write to some degree but the mother usually wrote the notes. Sometimes the father could neither read nor write. Most parents seemed to have regarded their children's incapacity as somewhat of a nuisance which was the fault of the schools and which, anyway, was outside *their* control. And there are indeed aspects of school life where the social background of the child affects his relationships with his peers and which are very largely controlled by the example of the teaching staff.

One such experience of the pain a child may experience from the thoughtless remarks of an incompetent teacher is clearly illustrated in the following account:

Mum and Dad had no problems, my brothers and sisters were younger and never felt the move such as I did. They never spoke real Northern as I did. When we moved here, instead of the teachers saying, 'Sorry, Clare, you don't pronounce it like that', it was a smack on the ear. To me this was dreadful. One teacher used to say: 'If you can't speak, we will not have foreigners in this classroom.' We were called foreigners! I used to go crying and come home crying – to me it was hell. School was hell. When I got home I used to say to my mother, '*I've been worried again and called "pig"*' (parents involved in animal husbandry).

In answer to the question 'Were you good at games?' one student described the confusion caused by two teachers discussing her in her presence:

Oh yes, I was all right there – I was; I felt very inferior because I was such a little girl, I was so thin. I remember the teacher coming round, they were doing a play and in this play there was a poor weakling of a little girl wanted. I heard her say something to the other teacher. One looked at the other, and pointed to me! I thought I would like that part, but then, it was only about half-a-dozen lines. I could not read it – so as it happened I was in the dancing thing. *As for the other girls, they all had boy friends and were interested in make-up and that sort of thing and I looked 11!*

Most of the men who could join in games quite liked school. One athletic student said:

Well, I liked school but I never learnt a lot.

but some men, usually those from other areas or undersized as children, found their peers unsympathetic, and there was little that teachers could do to help in such situations. As one student recalled:

> Originally I started off, and the family in London and I was just – just went to the infants for a couple of weeks before we went. Then we moved to a village and that was a completely different world. Quite honestly, it frightened me to death. I realised that I was only a little chap with a broad cockney accent and they used to take the biggest rise out of me going. This is going back some 25 years – you know. They had not been out of the village, half of them. I got to the point where I would not go to school if I did not have to.

Most students experienced not only the normal difficulties of growing up with their fellows at school, but also some form of a feeling of inferiority as they were unable to compete in the literacy discourse essential to the classroom. Marked as slow, dunces or whatever, they developed ways of getting on with their peers, by trying hard at games, or by leading or subscribing to the school's awkward element, or by simply agreeing to bother nobody provided they were left alone. To nearly all, their lot at school was, like the policeman's, not a happy one.

The students' present homes ranged from the executive estate property to ordinary council houses. Without exception, the homes visited were extremely ship-shape and tidy. And without exception, where the students had young children they were determined that their children should be able to read and write, and one would notice a couple of children's books lying around.

The total impression was of upwardly socially mobile *families*. Male students were encouraged by their wives, or by daughters who were secretaries.

> I said, 'I'm not going now' – that was a Monday! 'No, you are not getting me there!' So my *daughters* pushed me out of the house, more or less, and *we* went. When I got there it was all right.

So far as the female students were concerned, the husband was usually encouraging but not pressing and the wife took the initiative either to keep up with her husband or to start an independent career. There was no doubt that the increasing movement of wives to work, the increasing opportunities for women at work and the breakdown of marriages all combined to increase the pressure on the women to improve their literacy skills. One was struck by the large proportion of women over 40 among those interviewed, who were facing the need to fend for themselves after the breakdown of their marriage. One tutor described her student as:

> a lady in her mid-forties. How on earth she did it I shall never know! But she conducted her own divorce proceedings – she can read, but very slowly – she can't even write the cheques.

Nearly seven out of 10 students could decode three-letter words or four-letter words; four out of 10 could encode simple sentences in script. Only one out of 10 could write little more than their name; about a half ranged from printing words to printing simple sentences. In eight out of 10 cases, their knowledge was highly eccentric in that they could decode and encode complex words here and there and be quite stymied with simple words. Of those who could write, a large proportion made spelling mistakes which were, according to their form of pronunciation, perfectly reasonable and the very variation in skills within each individual suggests that the schools attempted and succeeded in drilling in some words. What they failed to do was to establish patterns in the students' minds.

Emerging patterns

From this general survey certain patterns emerge, namely, that:
(a) our sample consists of students who failed and knew that early in their primary school life, at about the age of eight or nine. Moreover, they knew they were oddities; the other 99 per cent seemed to get along;
(b) nearly all of the students lacked even the most basic home literary provision;
(c) many of the students knew of the frustration of their parents with the school; a few actually witnessed a parent/teacher row;
(d) the form of remedial tuition in the secondary schools, whilst no doubt successful with some children, had little effect on our student sample. If anything, the further efforts in the secondary school merely confirmed their sense of failure in that respect; but
(e) the schools, particularly the secondary schools, did give them enough confidence and sometimes other skills to cope with those aspects of life where literacy is not required. If the schools are to blame to some extent for the lack of literacy skills, they nevertheless deserve some credit for their general educative effort;
(f) most of the schools, primary and secondary, attempted some form of remedial work; therefore, if the students did not learn then, it would be highly optimistic to expect marked results in less than

three to four years in adult tuition, except in the cases where social circumstances led to non-attendance. A classic case of this is that of the student who said:

Every time they wanted to send us to school, they moved the caravan. We kept moving about. Nobody said anything to them about attending school. Isn't it marvellous? You would not get away with it now, would you? I would not want my children to get away with it!

Consequently during their school life the students began to develop alternate methods for coping and various systems for disguising their inadequacies. Essential words were usually learnt by rote.

I never told the driving instructor I could not read! I asked him what questions what I got to be asked. I got my Mum to read them to me, then I 'read' to her. When he came to do it that was it. ('Good memory, then?') Yes.

Others developed their own form of shorthand. Similarly, evasion techniques were developed starting from avoiding English lessons, behaving correctly if left alone and so on.

('How did you get by?') *It's a knack* – I just know it or I say I'll find out. I don't know how I do it but I've been doing it for *nineteen* years and getting away with it. *I hope you don't think I've been cheating anybody!* Some of my closest friends still don't know.

Most of the students were eminently sensible and realistic about their problem, as the evidence of the following three students suggests:

(a) I say you don't have to read a book to use a shovel – you see. You don't read a book to ride a bike.
(b) I'm good at my job!
(c) My employer knew – he could not care less!

Nonetheless to others their lack of ability can affect their social lives cruelly. One student described his experience when he took his driving test:

I was terrified when I took my test because I had to memorise everything – it's always with you, sometimes you notice it more than other times.

Thus, the students who came forward had learned various techniques of survival and all had managed efficiently enough to come, largely through the support of their families, for further tuition. They are the aristocrats of the educationally under-privileged, handicapped by lack of a particular skill but unbowed. How they came to be so is to describe the human condition, and no single simple cause seems to be identifiable. What is clear is that very few indeed are scholarly, most want to better themselves, very few indeed come from the socially multidisadvantaged where the weight of daily problems gradually saps hope and effort.

These students entered into a learning arrangement with a tutor; what were these relationships and how did they develop? Were they conducive to student achievement?

IV Tutor-student relationships

The tutors' views

It is generally agreed that the performance of children usually rises to fulfil the expectations of their teachers. Apparently this is also true of adults. Morgan (1977), a senior tutor in adult literacy education in Mid-Glamorgan in Wales, wrote:

> Sometimes they (volunteer tutors) become so involved with their student that they *will not accept* that their student falls short of the norm. I've a feeling that this kind of faith rubs off on to the student and works to his advantage.

However, this can only occur if the tutor's expectations are reasonably founded. Analysis of the evidence on student/tutor relationships summarised, mainly through key quotations, in this chapter reveals some of the pitfalls in the mutual adjustment process.

Tutors were asked to comment on their expectation of the type of student they thought they might have assigned to them and their own personal view of the characteristics of a 'good' tutor in the field of adult literacy.

The type of student expected

In an ideal world it would have been possible to question tutors before they had met their students, but in the event tutors could only be contacted for interview after they had taught their student for some time. Therefore their evidence must be to some degree vitiated by:

(a) the stereotype illiterate adult in the media, television programmes, radio series and newspaper articles, and booklets which tutors had already noted;

(b) the descriptions of typical students given in training schemes; and
(c) their own experience of students to date.

Nevertheless, most tutors attempted to cast their minds back and quite often their original expectations were described implicitly by noting what surprised them later. In these terms, a tutor organiser said:

> The most amazing thing about them is how nice they all are. How polite, not forced politeness, a natural politeness.

The suggestion is of an expectation of uncouthness assumed to derive, no doubt, from an inability to read.

Another tutor revealed her preconceptions in a similar vein:

> I was surprised to find such an age range and the fact that most of them were male.

Here the tutor seems to have expected that the students coming forward would be representative of the male/female balance in the population at large and that presumably the demand for literacy would be associated with some form of age group motivation, perhaps, for example, recent school leavers seeking to qualify themselves for better employment. Despite media assertions that most students were of average intelligence but fortuitously lacking in a particular skill, the greatest proportion of tutors expected a slow, perhaps slow-witted, person.

> I expected, quite honestly, to be confronted with a load of half-wits, I really did. Not at all the type of people who come. I thought you would have to be a half-wit not to be able to read the front page of the *Daily Mail*.
>
> Yes, I was expecting to find somebody less competent, possibly suffering from dyslexia. I was expecting less intelligent people; I did not know whether they were mentally retarded or not.
>
> I was prepared for anything so I have not been surprised. I expected them to be worse than they are. I have been surprised at how intelligent they are because you almost began to think that perhaps these people are idiots not to have learnt!
>
> I thought I might get someone who would find it slow and difficult – but I have not had to deal with anyone right from the beginning.
>
> I was surprised because I expected someone slower, but there is hardly any need to revise. He remembers!
>
> I expected a man to begin with – not a woman. I was very surprised at her intelligence.

Tutors were taken aback at both the normality of their students and, in many cases, their prior skill in literacy. Their evidence suggests that many of them had in mind a poor soul who would not really go very far but who would be able to grasp, within limitations, some of the basic skills. The impression is of an act of kindness on a par with the deed of replacing fledglings in a nest. If this is so, then it is reasonable to suppose that many tutors would have a shattering experience, and indeed this was the case.

> She is very aware; when she knows what is required, she will do it. She is a manipulator and a survivor. She does not do what her teacher says but rather what she (herself) wants.

One tutor had an unnerving experience:

> I did not expect this type. I think it is a very difficult situation. I am not a teacher and I have only experience of my own children. I would never, ever contemplate teaching a child now because I feel I could do so much damage. It is his misfortune. I would teach my own children but I don't think I would contemplate teaching anybody else's children.

One of the influences on tutor expectation was the tutor's conception of the adequacy of the school system. Quite a few tutors did not expect older people because they assumed that illiterate adults resulted from what they considered to be the contemporary phenomenon of inadequate teaching.

> I was surprised at that (the student's age) because if this had happened to a 20-year-old, I would have said it was the modern way of teaching where they let their imagination go and they are more concerned with creative writing.

> There are a lot of people getting through our loopholes, I expected younger people.

and:

> There are very anti-teacher public feelings at the moment. I feel sure that the pendulum is swinging very fast indeed – one dare talk about grammar again. It's no longer a dirty word. I would put a great deal on the non-reading problems – they should sit down every day and read and read; it's boring and tedious for the teacher and that is where the trouble lies! They are not prepared to do it.

Other tutors displayed the same lack of faith in the school system. Two major points arise from their evidence. First, the expectations of the literacy tutors were much affected by the general climate of opinion, for this was the period when the so-called 'Great Education Debate' was inaugurated. Second, the tutors felt that the students had been let down by the school teachers, so that their task was a rather simple one of rectifying the omissions. Consequently the tutors' expectation of student potential achievement would be optimistic rather than realistic: on the other hand, in many cases a preconceived underestimate of general ability; on the other, an overestimate of the ease of remedial tuition with adults.

As tutors acquired experience of teaching a student, realism filtered through:

> I have heard the comment that students are above average but I am not sure whether this is so, as a generalisation. I think I was prepared for either of the students I had. But they constitute, between them, an enormous range of ability.

However, it must be recorded that although the majority of tutors underwent a major educational experience, the students often paid a high price. One tutor, in a period of six months, remarked, as follows, about four students who had passed through her hands:

First student: 'Then suddenly he said he had a lot of work to do, and I lost him!'

Second student: 'After a couple of months another young man came, for a couple of weeks or so, from round the corner, which is a notorious slum area. But I've never heard any more from him!'

Third student: 'Then I had a young woman who came for some weeks and then stopped!'

Fourth student: 'Then something happened, she was ill and so on, and I've not seen her for months and months. . . .'

The teacher was an experienced teacher with specific experience of teaching literacy skills in secondary schools. The hypothesis is that she could be expected to have a more realistic assessment of the adult illiterate than a non-specialist volunteer. Thus it may appear that the realistic expectations of experienced teachers who become tutors of adults may be a bar to achievement. This point is worth some further development, for the tutor in question said:

I think that I have got on well with all the students; the second one, of course, I never really saw, the fourth did actually come. The first one was very enthusiastic, a sweet girl; the third one never said why she left. The fourth one may have dropped out for a time.

Thus the tutor felt that she was getting along well with the students, and it has been argued that because she was a teacher her expectations of her students' potential ability would be accurate. But, in fact, the fourth student's evidence clearly shows that her tutor's expectations were too demanding:

I had about half-a-dozen times with my tutor. She goes a little bit *too fast* for me – *she thinks I'm better than I am.* She is so nice and so patient. It's the endings of words, I could not hear any difference between one and the other. They were spelt differently but, to me, they were the same, so how do I know. She said, 'Well, you do know or you don't.' So I said, 'Well, I just don't!' There is no quick way, is there? It's a long job. Quite honestly, when I have cooked for seven and put my children to bed – quite honestly, I do, as a rule, feel very tired.

There lies the kernel of the problem: most of the tutors specifically thought of various degrees of literacy skills when they contemplated taking on their adult students. Very few, whether trained teachers or not, in describing expectations, considered the possibility of a human being with problems, only one of which was literacy. This stemmed largely from the concentration, in the early stages of the adult literacy campaign, on questions of literacy skills. The achievement of most of the tutors was their willingness to learn, and learn quickly, that they were dealing with a human problem and thus expectations were rapidly revised. One of the tutors rather movingly described this process of reassessment:

No, I did not know what to expect or what type of pupil I would have. It boils down to – that you get the pupil who lives near to you. I phoned her up and she came to see me. We both admitted that we did not know where to go from there. We talked it over, and the next week we started on her problem. It would have worried me to think about the sort of pupil I would have. When I was told it was a spelling problem, I knew where to start. You are given a resumé of their attempts at the test and what goes on in the discussion (with the organiser). You are not completely in the dark, but as I say, I have become very friendly with my pupil and right from the beginning! She is a great talker so that any one-hour lesson is never one hour. She comes about 7.30 and goes about 11. We talk, then we work, then have coffee and so we make an evening of it; which is a bit trying sometimes, but it is better to be on a good basis. I don't say I could be like this with all pupils! The only problems are odd words repeatedly wrong – it's a bit frustrating. It takes a long time, I wonder why she spells *people* correctly? She comes twice a week, she writes to me once a week; if she is away she sends it by post, if she is here, she brings it. It's good practice for her, getting pen to paper.

Thus, from a variety of sources, experience of school or of life, from the media, from training schemes, from talking to other tutors, each tutor had an idea, though sometimes extremely nebulous, of who would be their student. Sometimes this was extreme:

I was very surprised at the second one – an illiterate man! My guess of the typical would be the woman of 50, eight children, a gaudy dresser.

This Dickensian picture of an illiterate has an element of the *grande dame* approach about it and, indeed, this tutor after some experience remarked:

Some of their tutors do not realise that some people just won't make that much progress. You can't expect miracles; some tutors try too hard and kill enthusiasm.

Consequently tutor expectations and attitudes varied enormously and it is highly probable that those students who gave up after a short period of tuition did so not because they had reached a limited objective like learning the Highway Code, but because they could no longer stand their tutor's attitude. How would a student whose tutor described her as '50, eight children and gaudy dresser' deal with the situation, other than by quitting? The illustrations of expectations given above clearly show that many tutors were ill-prepared and some lack of achievement must be ascribed to this cause. But fortunately, preconceptions were jettisoned after the early meetings.

As it seemed that tutors' attitudes to their students could be largely influenced by their various notions of what were the characteristics of a 'good' tutor, tutors were asked for their views.

The characteristics of 'good' tutors

In the previous section the evidence relied on tutors' memories; this part deals with their judgement and, to quote La Rochefoucauld's maxim: 'Everyone complains of his memory but no one complains of his judgement.'

Perhaps the most outstanding feature of the tutors' opinions was the remarkable level of agreement. Asked what are the personal qualities of a good tutor, an organiser replied:

> Generosity in the widest sense of the word. Understanding and sympathy and the ability to be tough when the occasion arises. A modicum of intelligence – it does not need a lot. A wealth of common sense.

A tutor who had taught adults for a year, expressed the humility that is the characteristic of the inspired adult tutor:

> Somebody with not too fixed ideas on what somebody should be able to do. Adaptability, yes definitely. I just accept that they cannot read or that they are not very good at it. You just have to have immense patience – and try to help rather than sort of think, well, they should be able to read – they *must be able* to read and *I must make them*!

Other tutors underlined a basic minimum skill in teaching reading, though again, as the next quotation shows, human qualities were those most desired.

> Some understanding of reading. I do not think that one can proceed without some minimal understanding of reading. A sympathy for people – some people seem to have this ability to establish an empathy with people. Perhaps it is just that they listen. In a reading situation it is very difficult not to tell them everything and not to do everything. Sometimes it is more difficult just to be calm. I think you can tell people who are like this. Personality types – with calmness and patience. I think the commitment has to be fairly deep because you can come up against disappointments. So, the sort of person who can weather disappointment; this is important.

Another tutor enlarged on the opportunities given to tutors of adults, whilst at the same time reiterating the demanding nature of the work.

> The first is that they (tutors) like people – they have to like people. They have to be well educated themselves – broadly education, *not school educated.* It is often tiny seeds from your experience which

will give you the key to the student you are working with. Kindness plus patience. The students are very demanding; in fact, you have to sit there and *wait* for them to find it out. Things which were obvious to you and *easy* to you and to which you do not even give a second thought are very *new* to them. And this is something you have to work at.

The criterion 'empathy' would be expected, as would be that of 'adaptability' which was also mentioned frequently. What was perhaps surprising was the continual recurrence of the word 'patience'. Training courses which did not include some practical sessions were particularly prone to dwell on literacy techniques, although lecturers often took some trouble to describe how patient a tutor needed to be. Nevertheless, the impression remains that many tutors never realised quite how much patience was required, and the insistence of tutors on this quality as the most desirable of virtues surely suggests that practice concentrated their minds:

> Above all else patience – *above all else*. I found it quite incredible that with someone who appears to be quite bright, just to give an example, I spent two hours trying to teach him four lines. And we did read for *two solid hours these four lines*. At the end of it, I was not sure that he was any better equipped to read than when we started. I tried to teach him, as it was important *to him* to learn it off by heart. Funnily enough, when I walked in this time, I said, 'Right, out with your book and let's look at those four lines!' He could read them, and that's amazing!

Indeed, patience as a desirable personality trait was directly mentioned by nearly 70 per cent of the tutors. Adaptability came second, being mentioned by just over 40 per cent of the tutors, and 'a sense of humour' was frequently mentioned.

The qualities of a good tutor in adult education were summarised by a tutor organiser who said:

> I would like them to be sensitive most of all; that is most important – then they should be *bright and cheerful*. This encourages students to *come and stay*. (How often discussions concerning adult education ignore the ability of adults to stay away!) They should know how to spell themselves and have a *real interest in words and reading* and then they should be able to put that over and teach it.

The tutor organisers expected the tutors to impart knowledge and enthusiasm simultaneously while never seeming to impose authority;

the tutors themselves accepted these objectives but recognised the demands made on them in respect of patience and adaptability, and the evidence suggests that many tutor organisers did not appreciate the extent of these demands on part-time volunteer tutors.

Consequently the appreciation of the services of volunteer tutors tended to become the more optimistic as the witness was further up the organisational scale. This is patently a daunting assertion, for it implies, first, that tutors were, on the whole, ill-prepared to meet the demands of their students and, secondly, that to prepare volunteers properly, a lengthy training course with an extensive module of practical work was necessary, and, thirdly, that volunteers needed to be chosen whose daily work demands were not so strenuous as to make them somewhat impatient when taking their student at the end of the day. The evidence suggests that all these three propositions are true, and the following passage illustrates the case for saying so. It comes from a young, thoughtful and enthusiastic tutor who said he joined the scheme because:

> It's mainly to try and give people an interest in some of the things that I enjoy.

He said:

> One of the most important things is – the thing brought home to us on the *short induction course* we had – four weeks which was to my mind a bit of a waste of time, but perhaps to other people useful. An insistence that we regard these people as real people; the ability not to be afraid to establish a quite close relationship. The ability for a fairly deep concentration so you can see where their mistakes were being made, and to get right to the point of the problem and to start working on it. Because the student is not terribly aware of what is causing the difficulty, you have to be very sensitive and adaptable to see if they are making a similar kind of mistake and you can pinpoint it. But it may be that *that is not causing* the problem so you have to rethink it. And there are whole lessons where you are trying to get as close as you can to the mistakes which are coming up.

Interviewer: Do you find the work demanding?

Tutor: Yes, I do. I really notice it if I have had a bad day at work and I am feeling tired. Then I am not performing nearly as well. *It does take a lot out of you.* I do not want to overplay that too much and make it sound as though I am going on – it is just that you have to be on the ball all the time.

Interviewer: A good tutor has to have?

Tutor: Adaptability and patience – and – sympathy!

Thus it is argued that the whole basis of a scheme which assumed the availability of an army of effective practitioners, as distinct from well-intentioned volunteers, was based on a false premiss. The evidence is that, fortunately for this scheme, not too many students came forward so that the cohort of volunteer tutors who were used usually possessed the necessary qualities to become adult tutors. There is no doubt that further extensions of the literacy scheme on the original basis would have run up against the law of diminishing returns as far as suitable tutors were concerned.

Consequently the present study of criteria for success is based on an experience which fortuitously engaged those tutors whose enthusiasm was sufficient to sustain them in the face of demanding work. That this enthusiasm was usually present is shown by their replies to the next question: What made you take part in the adult literacy scheme? The answers to this question were usually that:

(a) the tutors were already teachers and therefore had an opportunity to extend their service to a wider population;

(b) the tutors felt a sense of social duty; or

(c) the tutors enjoyed literacy and wished to share in that enjoyment.

The following quotations are illustrative as typical answers within each of the above categories:

(a) I have a gift for teaching and thought I should make some return to society by helping adults.

As an aside the tutor also remarked:

I thought teaching adults would have a feedback which would help with teaching in schools.

As this was frequently mentioned by teachers in schools, it does appear that teachers welcomed the training schemes as a form of revision or voluntary attendance at an 'in-service' course.

(b) I heard of it from a Workers' Educational Association tutor who was appealing for tutors. In fact my father ran a Norfolk farm and he used to lend the barn to agricultural labourers who were learning to read and write in the 1890s.

(c) I was shocked at the thought of not being able to read because it is the first thing I do. When I have got five minutes, I read. You know, anything. I thought it must be terrible not to be able to read at all and so I phoned the organiser!

To gain a deeper insight into the tutors' attitudes, tutors were asked: What are the benefits you have gained from joining the scheme?

Tutors' views of the benefits to themselves

Many tutors found teaching an adult particularly rewarding:

He is so keen – a child does not know why he is reading – an adult knows!

Other tutors felt a sense of satisfaction from a feeling of participation in the student's progress:

The student's progress. After a student's setback, seeing him come back with confidence. As a matter of fact, he said last Monday that he had been offered another job.

It comes from visible progress *both* in personality and literacy skills. I doubt if one would get any satisfaction from teaching a student who did not make progress!

To other tutors, the opportunity to teach adults was a means to escape from the routine of housewifery:

I really enjoy it because I get away from the routine. I used to teach adult immigrants. It's *their* enthusiasm which helps you to carry on.

But other tutors considered that their satisfaction derived from the specific increase in the student's literacy skills, often because they described themselves as voracious readers, and others emphasised increases in confidence:

Personally, I get a very great deal of satisfaction – it's so important to be able to read and write.

Watching him make progress, particularly in confidence.

A general assessment of tutors' attitudes

The majority of tutors gained from indulging in an act of service and it is surely right and proper that they should derive satisfaction from the progress of their students. Nevertheless, 'virtue itself turns to vice, being misapplied', and some tutors were guilty of believing that students should always display courtesy and gratitude. For example, a young, unqualified and somewhat naïve tutor said:

> Satisfaction to the tutor? I think a person bothering to come or hand in written work, or being prepared to make alternative arrangements for a lesson. It is rather depressing when you say to a student, 'I cannot make it on Thursday, can you make it on Wednesday?' And they say, 'Oh, no! I'd better leave it for a week! Can you come in a fortnight?' That is depressing. Whereas, if something goes wrong and they immediately ring up and say, 'Could I come another night instead?' then you know they want to come and learn which is, to me, the most rewarding thing.

Moreover, as most tutors were women, there were examples of the exercise of maternalism or child substitution. Sometimes good tutors overstepped the mark, for example, in one case:

Tutor: I have had things like a letter arriving from the Court asking if he would do jury service and *I* decided that that was out of the question. Apart from any reading difficulties of any documents he might be required to see, I did not think that he would be able to concentrate a whole day. He is *not used to lengthy conversation* and I do not think that he would be able to manage it. He was worried; the first time, in fact, that he was worried about being embarrassed by his difficulty in reading. He told me quite early on that the people he worked with knew because I asked him if I could phone him at work and he said, 'Oh, there is no problem about that!'

Student: Oh, yes! *I want to get more independent than I am already.* One likes to be independent so it is necessary to have another tutor (present tutor leaving area). It may be hard for me to find some as good – yes, she was very dedicated.

Similarly, as just over 40 per cent of the tutors were school teachers, or had been so, the 'school' attitude sometimes emerged. One tutor, after several attempts to persuade the student to pronounce *ch*, finally burst forth: 'ch, ch, ch – as in choo-choo'. The expression on the face of that burly lorry-driver's mate defies description.

Through the answers to the above questions, it is possible to identify three main periods in the development of student-tutor relationships as seen by the tutors, namely:

(a) the induction period
(b) the reactive period
(c) the professional period.

(a) *The induction period*

This period includes the decision to offer their services, the training period and the build-up of expectations. The relatively short time-scale allowed to prepare the tutor force before the expected results of the BBC information broadcasts scheduled for October 1975 inevitably led to rather rushed training schemes. Furthermore, the decision to engage volunteers suggests that training demands on their time should rarely exceed 10 or 12 hours. Consequently, as shown above, tutor expectations ranged from the realistic to the bizarre and in the light of some of the expectations recorded, it is surprising that some student-tutor relationships lasted beyond one meeting. Indeed, some did not. Nevertheless, most tutors persevered and most pairs entered the reactive period, though this happened more often where tutors were paired in a room supervised by a tutor-organiser than in the case of pairs operating in domestic establishments.

(b) *The reactive period*

It was in this period, usually within the first six weeks, that most pairs decided to continue together either to learn the literacy skills or to become friends or to part. To many tutors this was a period of sheer trauma:

> I lost my first student after six lessons and rather lost my nerve. In his case he had a wife who had been to a grammar school before she was married and had been a secretary to a solicitor. I said, 'Surely she would be a better help?' It was very difficult to arrange a time for him to come because he had so many occupations and he just did not realise how much time he would have to give up.

Some tutors were able to share common experiences with their students and built up a relationship on this basis:

> I came into teaching late in life; I had considerable industrial experience. We can talk about common experiences; we also discuss measurements as used in industry which has probably made a difference; but, of course, personalities come into it.

In many cases, during this reactive period, students experienced a plateau of learning, and on reaching this many students left or changed their relation with the tutor to one of friendship in which literacy tuition was a minor by-product. Sometimes the plateau of learning was associated with what one tutor called 'the circumstances of life', but whatever the cause, this period of 'no progress' was a testing one for both student and tutor.

Indeed, for most tutors, the ability to get through the reactive period depended on progress and yet many tutors, as we have shown in earlier chapters, had no notion of the criteria for student achievement and therefore no yardstick by which to measure progress. Those tutors who were solely concerned with literacy skill achievement were particularly at a disadvantage, but it is clear that many were, in fact, actually making tremendous progress in building up the students' confidence. Yet they often seemed, during the interviews, to fall back on the diffident phrase, 'Well, I suppose he is more confident.' Thus, it could be argued that at least some failures during the 'reactive' period were due to the tutors' lack of awareness of the criteria of achievement.

But fortunately, most tutors struggled on and showed a willingness to abandon teaching strategies that clearly were not working and to adopt fresh ones. This characteristic cannot be over-appreciated for, in practice, the range of the students' skill abilities made it extremely difficult for training schemes to generalise. In one case the student:

> enjoys reading and enjoys writing. You see she writes a lot for me. *As it was a spelling problem. . . .*

But, unfortunately, that was only part of the problem. An impending divorce suit and other problems emerged and the tutor's role altered swiftly to that of confessor rather than pedagogue.

Where the tutor was experienced, the 'reactive period' was not one of high drama but one of cool assessment. One such tutor was able to see her student realistically and in the round:

> Candidly, my personal view is that I have not made much progress with him. I think I have been more of a psychological prop to him than anything else. I think I've given him confidence because he felt, at school, that he had been written off as dim-witted – which he obviously is not – and, more than anything, I have given him a certain amount of *self-confidence*. He had made a certain amount of reading progress; I reckon his reading age is 10 or 11 by my rather simple test. I think it was seven or eight when he started. I find he regresses enormously if there is any period when I do not see him.

The sheer degree of adaptability of some tutors during this period was quite astonishing:

But massaging his feet did make a difference, although I only did this for a few times. The first difference I noticed was the words they get on 'On the Move' programmes, because he was watching these. He did not remember anything of it, but he watched them and liked the programmes. He enjoyed them and thought they helped him. So I said: 'Write down the word in your notebook.' Not only did he do that but he found three more words which rhymed with it. This is only since I've been doing his feet, he could not have done it before – removes tension, you know!

(c) *The professional period*

Thus, by practical experience tutors moved into the third stage of their relationships with their students, the professional period. The characteristic of this period, which may be one of years rather than months, is a maturity of relationship, based on equality and a common determination to succeed. The tutor now had a grasp of the technicalities of using linguistic methods and resource materials and a clearer understanding of the aims of adult education. One tutor described how her student reached a plateau learning period at the end of about six months' tuition. She said that she simply gave a tremendous amount of praise for each correct word during the lesson, and at the end of the lesson she also switched to games such as 'Scrabble'. Gradually, six weeks later, the student responded and asked to write a story with her help. There was a professional flavour in this account which comes from an elderly tutor originally trained as a 'Froebel' teacher.

However good the tutor, unless the student played his part there would be little achievement; thus, the students' expectations and experiences are the subject of the next section.

Students' views of tutor-student relationships

The students that were seen were those whose tutors agreed could be interviewed. This in itself implied that the tutor was confident that a sufficiently close relationship had been established to allow for the intervention of a third person. In view of this limitation, it is likely that those students not interviewed experienced greater difficulties, and thus the picture that emerges probably represents the more successful aspects of the literacy schemes. Furthermore, most of the students in the sample were grateful to their tutors and uncommonly polite. In addition, most students, by definition, were unaware of the pedagogical niceties of teaching literacy and quite ready to accept any programme of tuition. Thus, the hardest evidence of their satisfaction with their relationship must lie in their continued attendance and there is a strident statistic in that, between establishing original contact with the tutors and making arrangements for tuition, one-quarter of the students had opted out. But after this early winnowing process, it appeared that those students who continued attended regularly for long periods. This is particularly true of those students paired with tutors and receiving tuition under the supervision of an organiser/tutor. In these terms, students, like the tutors, experienced the same three broad periods in the establishment of their relationship: the induction period, the reactive period and the professional period.

The introduction of an illiterate student to a scheme usually occurred through the visual media, his wife, his doctor, his children's school teacher, or social service officials. Written material, by definition, rarely directly attracted the illiterate student, but those students who could read enough would have seen a newspaper advertisement of the type that, if you need help with reading or spelling, contact a telephone number. This fact is of major importance, for at times the visual media struck a highly optimistic note about the difficulties. Similarly, friends or relations persuading students to join would be encouraging to a degree which rather underestimated the amount of sheer hard labour involved in their studies. The newspaper advertisements emphasised the word 'help', and the response was often to an offer of *help* as such. Consequently many students expected a quick conversion course, of no greater difficulty than learning to drive a car. Many thought it would be rather like school, but this time things would be different; they would learn because they had their own special individual tutor.

They shaved, washed, put on their best clothes and presented themselves. While many recalled their first meeting as evoking a sense of trepidation laced with bravado, most of those interviewed argued that it was like joining any new club or society. Nearly all students were seen by the local organiser for the initial meeting; thereafter those students studying in domestic establishments were put solely in the hands of their individual tutor, but those with a tutor in a class under the supervision of the tutor/organiser continued the initial relationship with the tutor/organiser. For this reason there was a clear dichotomy in the two types of provision: in the first, the relationship of the students was a developing one between two adults; in the second, the relationship of the student was a three-cornered one between himself, his tutor and his tutor/organiser.

One of the most interesting facets of this latter type of relationship was that, without exception, the student regarded the tutor/organiser as equivalent to or *more important* than his paired tutor. This had two effects: first, a disagreement with the paired tutor could be solved by appeal to the tutor/organiser, and, secondly, the emotional involvement was less because the tutor/organiser, who was *always* there, dealt indirectly with the student, and the paired tutor, who would often be away or be switched to another student, was *never always* there. As a consequence of these relationships, it was very rare to hear any student refer to his 'home' tutor in less than superlatives, whereas the paired tutor would be criticised, though it was made clear that this criticism did not apply to the tutor/organiser. Therefore the students' evidence tended to be biased according to the type of tuition he was receiving, and often the self-criticism of the 'home' tutor was the more valuable evidence of the student's point of view than that of the student: thus a 'home' student's evidence was often interpreted after comparison with his tutor's comments and the evidence of each group is given separately in the following sections.

The 'home'-based students

(a) *The induction period*
Usually the decision to join a scheme was taken after a long gestation period:

> Really it has been a build-up over a number of years. You know I have always been conscious that I was unable to spell. My reading was reasonable – I had often said to my wife, I must go and see if I could find a private tutor or somebody.

Nevertheless, the actual decision to join was the result of personal support from an interested friend or relation:

> *She* (his wife) read it out of the paper and asked if I would be interested. *She* phoned up Mrs. A, who came on Monday morning. She gave me some little tests and said she would get me a tutor. Mr. B (the prospective tutor) phoned up on Monday afternoon, but I did not have the car because my wife was using it for her work, so I walked over to Mr. B and I have been with him ever since.

Thus, most students met their tutor in a state of some excitement and anticipation; Mr. B's student, for example, had just walked eight miles on an afternoon when he usually slept to prepare for the night shift. Most tutors remarked on their students' initial nervousness; 'he perspired', 'he shook like a leaf' were phrases that recurred, and the situation was one of heightened tension and each individual tutor was expected to cope. It appeared that some tutors at this stage had doubts about their ability to deal with particular students; similarly, some students hinted that they too wondered if they had reached the right person. But though students were assured of their rights to change tutors, it seems that most were so relieved to find a tutor at all that the idea of changing tutors seemed to be a polite formula. Indeed, most students weathered the original two meetings; after that there appears to have been on the part of the students a process of reassessment, that is, a reactive period.

(b) The reactive period

During the reactive period students assessed what the tutors required of them and their ability and willingness to meet those requirements. It was in this period that students took the decision to disengage, sometimes because they found the tutor's personality incompatible, more often because they found the level of work too demanding, and frequently because the tutor was unable to handle the psychological rebound from the first flush of enthusiasm. Sometimes the student sensed that the tutor herself was disappointed.

The students' processes of disengagement tended to be ritualised; excuses were offered which students felt would be least offensive to tutors. Perhaps the saddest thing of all was that many of the students who disengaged identified their tutor with the whole literacy scheme. Few sought other tutors.

The inadequacies of tutors working by themselves emerged too often to inspire confidence in this system. For example, though many agreed that tuition should be student-interest-centred or student-work-centred, many tutors had little idea of the students' work.

> I was not certain about what he did. I think he was a driver of some sort.

Yet all the students who were interviewed talked freely about their work.

Whenever the tutor was unaware that the student was reacting as much to her as she was to him, the student usually left. Nevertheless about four in 10 tutors and students settled down, established good relationships and modes of tuition, adjusted to their roles and passed on to the 'professional' period. Some students never reached this stage but settled for friendship.

(c) The professional period

Usually this occurred after six months; it was characterised by a quiet routine of tuition. At its best the student gained a sense of independence and used his newly acquired skills in the course of his daily life.

Students who felt that they had reached this stage were quite prepared to change tutors if their first tutor left the area. But more often than not students used their newly acquired skills with their tutor: it appeared that the one-to-one system, through isolation, emphasised the feeling of well-being with, and loyalty to, a particular tutor. One student expressed her desire for a personal tutor and extreme privacy very forcibly:

> You put me in a class of five other people who cannot spell and I would not be here today. I would curl up. I don't know why I feel it. There are only certain people I could accept as a tutor – fortunately we have made friends.

But is this the best type of tuition to help such a student? As an initial introduction to a scheme it may, perhaps, have some merit but in the long run the student may not have broken out of her isolation. On the other hand, when this relationship is successful and the tuition is appropriate, this system succeeds and succeeds brilliantly.

It is, perhaps, these outstanding successes that have led to too optimistic a view of this type of system as a whole. The winnowing effect on student numbers of the inductive and reactive periods must always be kept in mind. Strong motivation in the student and compatibility between the student and the tutor appeared to be essential factors in such successes. One student described reading to his two-and-a-half year old girl:

> I read it, then she asks me questions and answers them and looks at the pictures and that. I am pleased with myself. That I can read and talk to her. At work I had to fill in forms – I always had to ask somebody and I felt embarrassed about it. Now I am beginning. I don't have to ask anybody. I feel I can do it now. And I get it correct now.

But even this student who got on so well with his tutor and who was obviously making distinct progress, had to seek support from a third person:

> At about the end of six months I had a little difficulty – then I saw this thing on telly ('On the Move') – a student talking about his experience – *and that put me back on to it again.*

The paired students under tutor/organiser supervision

(a) *The induction period*
As in the case of the 'home'-based students, the majority of these

students took some time in making up their minds to join. Usually they joined this organisation because they had no idea of alternatives; but a few had tried 'home'-based tutors and opted for classes and a few had deliberately chosen either the class or the 'home'-based system. A typical experience of joining is as follows:

> Well, a couple of years or so, I thought it was about time I did something for my reading and writing. But I never got round to it. Her mentioning it (girl friend) – she made the final arrangement with the (Principal of the Adult Education Centre). I had notification of when the first course was on and I did not come the first week. So she (girl friend) came round and got me out of the house. I was, I was shoved in. Yes, literally, shoved in the door.

The principal then took him up to the classroom and introduced him to the tutor/organiser who after a brief chat introduced him to a tutor. The tutor talked about matters which interested him and started the tuition. In an hour he was enjoying the coffee-break and had met 'fellow sufferers'.

(b) *The reactive period*
This period seems fairly easy for the student as tutors are switched by the organiser if a tension is being built up. On one occasion a student was halted at the door by the tutor/organiser and given a new tutor; all this occurred in a period of some 40 seconds. Asked in the coffee-break what happened, the student replied:

> I could not stand that man – spoke to me as if I was in school – the new tutor is all right and knows what she is doing.

Nevertheless, whatever the system, students may fail:

Interviewer (to student who had been a member of the class for four years): How many people dropped out?
Student: Yes, I know several who have dropped out.
Interviewer: Why?
Student: Not interested. Impatience. They thought that *in a matter of months*, they thought it was going to be over. Well that is my impression. It's the trouble, the routine of coming. Now I can read the paper and that sort of thing. You have to wash and change and make yourself have to except (give up) looking at the telly. Come in by seven o'clock! Well, there is a push to do that. Two nights? Exactly!

(c) *The professional period*

In this context this tends to come fairly early in most students' experience; perhaps the main reason is that students meet, from the very beginning, fellow students. The early tensions, thought to be a singular personal experience, become relieved when shared. The understanding that there is not one single tutor places the system on a more professional basis from the point of view of the student; at the same time there is the tutor/organiser providing continual support.

But this argument is often rejected by the supporters of single, personal tutor systems; they assert that one tutor is the essential personal help. But some *students* did not find it so:

> They stipulated that it was seven to nine but it was a question of how long a tutor would give you. So therefore my tutor would arrive at seven and say at eight o'clock 'Well, I must go!' So you only got three-quarters of an hour. No coffee at all – no break. *I found it very impersonal.* You each had a tutor which was nice, I suppose, in a way. Because you got the individual attention. But that was the only person you spoke to the whole time you were there!

Thus two points emerge:

(a) Whatever the system, good tutor/student relationships are extremely important factors in establishing achievement, but the evidence suggests that these will be strengthened if there are opportunities for the development of good student-student relationships.

(b) Tutors have to be thoroughly prepared and trained to be able to develop these relationships to the 'professional level'.

The term 'professional level' implies that tutors will have clear criteria of the aims and objectives of the exercise, for without those aims they are likely to behave somewhat like a rocket without a guidance system. In the following chapters the achievements of students will be examined to identify the appropriate criteria of success.

Assessment of the evidence collected

During the period October 1975 to May 1976, 49 tutors and 35 students were interviewed for the first time. During the period February to May 1977, these tutors and students were traced and, whenever possible, interviewed for a second time.

Of the 49 *tutors* previously interviewed:

(a) 26 had been teaching their students individually at home, and
(b) 23 had been teaching their students individually but were in a group under the supervision of a tutor/organiser.

Of the 26 in group (a) above, by 1977:

(i) four tutors had moved away from the area;
(ii) one had died;
(iii) one had become an organiser/interviewer;
(iv) one refused to co-operate further and refused to give any information.

All the rest of these tutors commented on their students' progress or otherwise, so that 19 recordings of second interviews were available.

The tutors in group (b) proved to be difficult to match against individual students because of the practice of using them as aides who, as a matter of policy, did not remain with any one student for a long period. However, because the students were in groups, the tutor/organiser continuously monitored the students' progress and consequently the achievements of each of those students still in these schemes were described by three tutor/organisers and by two tutor-aides who, for special reasons, had been allocated a particular student.

Of the 35 *students* previously interviewed:

(a) 16 were receiving tuition at home, and
(b) 19 were receiving tuition in groups under the supervision of a tutor/organiser.

Of the 16 in (a) above, by 1977:

(i) one had joined a local authority-organised group;
(ii) one was untraceable;
(iii) six were interviewed for a second time;
(iv) eight had ceased to have tuition for one reason or another.

Of the 19 students in (b) above, by 1977:

(i) two had ceased to have tuition for one reason or another;
(ii) four were on holiday or had moved to another centre, or did not turn up on the date arranged for interview;
(iii) 13 were interviewed for a second time.

Thus, *most* of the *tutors* who were re-interviewed had had a student

who had been taught at home, and *most students* who were re-interviewed had been taught as part of a group. But since the tutor/
organisers of the groups were the more experienced, on the whole,
their evidence could be regarded as carrying more weight.

Moreover, as the remarks of the sample of students from the home
tuition pairs agreed with the comments of the other students being
taught in groups, their aggregated perceptions of achievement could
be said to provide a legitimate basis for acceptable argument.

In the course of the first interviews, students and tutors talked
about their background, their achievements and their aims. The second
interviews were concerned solely with their perceptions of aims and
achievements but had the advantage of perspective. Recordings from
all sets of interviews were used as the raw data for analysis and interpretation. Some tutors who had taken on new students since the first
series of interviews were asked to comment on the progress of their
new students as well, so that the tutors' descriptions now contained
data based on their combined experience of about 100 students and
their evidence was, therefore, more authoritative on two counts:
namely, that the number of students was greater and that the tutors'
experience was longer.

Nevertheless there were more recordings of comments from tutors
than from students and it could be argued that tutors would tend to
perceive their activities in a favourable light and that the evidence
would, therefore, be skewed to give a 'halo' effect. In fact, this was not
the case. Tutors were extremely self-questioning, and concerned to
reach a true appreciation of what they had achieved. One tutor who
was not a trained teacher, in a covering letter containing samples of her
student's written work, wrote:

> Jack does not think tuition has helped his work very much, but
> he can now fill in his own timesheet.
>
> He is now able to use a telephone and his home life, he thinks,
> has improved. He now says that he will have a real go and work
> hard at it.
>
> As he has had two lapses of nine months each, one cannot
> say what the effect of continual study might have had. Also, he
> did no homework. He gets very tired and it all seems very difficult
> for him.

This passage illustrates the realism of the tutors' assessments in general;
it rings true.

Another reason for being impressed by the tutors' integrity arose
from their general demand that the evidence should be published. One
of the surprises was the frequency of the following typical conversation:

Interviewer: Well, thank you for all your help.

Tutor: What are you going to do now?

Interviewer: Write it up.

Tutor: Good. One thing! No whitewash and make sure it is published.

Interviewer: Yes, I'll do that.

Tutor: I am so fed up with each educational experiment being a total success. It is not so! Some parts are successful, other parts are complete failures. If only people would say so, we would all learn something useful and be in a better position next time. So you do that and I will not have wasted my time!

There was yet a further reason for accepting the accuracy of the tutors' evidence. Several students provided samples of their written work and this was shown to two independent panels of adjudicators. The comments of the adjudicators about the written work of particular students was, without exception, similar to that of the comment of the tutor or tutor/organiser.

Together these different strands of evidence confirmed, in general, the interviewer's impression of the integrity and the honesty of the tutors' approach to the evaluation of their students' progress; and thus the accuracy, in aggregate, of both tutors' and students' perceptions of the progress made was deemed to be methodologically acceptable.

V Affective personal achievements

The pervasiveness of 'confidence' as a criterion of success

In Chapter II, five major criteria of achievements were described and finally ranked as:

1   Affective personal achievements
2   Cognitive achievements
3   Enactive achievements
4   Socio-economic achievements
5   Affective social achievements.

However, in the interviews these terms were not used. Tutors and students used the currency of ordinary language; but, on occasion, they would be asked to place their perceptions in order. Starting with the original data, as the ethological approach demands, one tutor who had emphasised teaching the skills of reading and writing, *after the experience of a year*, replied quite firmly to a series of structured questions, as follows:

Interviewer: So really, putting it in order, what she gained was (a) confidence?

Tutor: Yes.

Interviewer: (b) Increase in spelling ability?

Tutor: Yes.

Interviewer: And it is really that order, is it?

Tutor: Yes, I think so. I think this *personal confidence thing is above everything else, really*. I would say that that applied generally, not only to her. With anyone, really.

And a student who had regularly attended, week by week, looking back, answered the question:

Interviewer: Now, if you took your reading and your writing and your feeling at ease with yourself, which would you put at the top?

Student: Well, the feeling better actually (with an apologetic glance at the tutor), and the next one the writing, and then the reading last.

Another tutor, who had also previously viewed her task as one of teaching skills, replied to the query 'So, putting his achievements in order . . .?':

Tutor: Confidence – number one! Sociability – number two! Enjoyment and pleasure – number three. *Then the skills* – that he can read being the most important of the skills.

The primacy of confidence in the scale of achievements emerged just as clearly in the description of a tutor responsible for matching students with other volunteer tutors:

Tutor: Yes, it has taken quite a lot of confidence – has it not – to come forward at all. And then, they are very nervous when I interview them. On the whole, extremely nervous. Then, you do see them more – entering the room with more confidence each time I go. I go once every three weeks to see how they are getting on.

Interviewer: So is that the basic thing?

Tutor: Yes.

Interviewer: After that comes the literacy skill improvements?

Tutor: Yes.

Most students also seem to realise in perspective that they gained something more than, and other than, skills:

Interviewer: What do you think you got out of it?

Student: Well, *I think confidence* really. It makes a difference; I am not shy in company now.

Interviewer: Would I be right if I put it in this order: confidence, spelling, grammar?

Student: Oh, yes! *Definitely the confidence* first.

And that student's evidence was confirmed by her tutor who, in explaining why both tutor and student had decided to bring the tuition to an end, said:

> She gained in confidence and ability. We thought that was enough. Beyond that there is nothing that I can really add. She has all her work. So she can show it to you when you see her.

Another tutor reported:

> My student is now taking a newspaper to work – *The Sun*; writing Christmas cards and reading the Literacy Project Magazine. I am very pleased with her progress. Those things measure it, in my mind. She *is very much more confident*.

Whilst the term 'confidence' was used by most tutors, particularly in the second interviews, as the best description of their students' most important achievement, the statement above illustrates that 'confidence' was not usually an isolatable achievement. It was the bedrock of all other achievements; it infused and inspired the other achievements. Though the greater the confidence, the more likely that the students would make greater progress in all the other aspects of achievement, it was also true that the student could gain in confidence but make no perceptible progress in the skills. Thus, some students made progress only in confidence.

The very pervasiveness of the concept of 'confidence' as a mark of progress, makes it necessary to analyse the constituents of the notion further and to place 'confidence' within the context of a series of criteria which, together, may be grouped under the phrase 'affective personal achievement'. Nonetheless, it is also clear that the affective personal achievements will be key factors in the progress in the other achievements. Conversely, lack of progress in the other achievements may be due to, and be evidence of, a fundamental lack of progress in confidence. To take an analogy from car driving, one may have the confidence to know that one may be able to drive a car, but without knowing about the gear system (cognitive progress), without practice (enactive achievement), without the funds or the persuasive power to obtain an instructor (socio-economic achievement) and without the ability to get along with a particular instructor or examiner (affective social achievement), one will never have the confidence actually to obtain a licence to drive a car, or the confidence to drive a car well.

Thus, the following analysis of confidence, and the discussion of what is meant by progress in confidence, deals with those factors of personality and of behaviour which indicate a basic individual attitude to the ability to *survive* in the environment in which the student is required to operate.

Confidence as evidenced by 'bearing'

One indicator of such behaviour was the evidence of a tutor who said '. . . entering a room with more confidence . . .' meaning that the student's bearing was now that of a person entering an environment which was becoming less alien to him; that the familiarity of environment increased his belief in a successful outcome and this was exemplified by a physical expressiveness. It could be assumed that because the environment was controlled by the scheme concerned with literacy skills, the student's bearing displayed a more positive attitude to his particular tutor and thereby towards the problem of literacy. But where, for teaching purposes, the student was a member of a social group, changes in his bearing might equally result from the mobility of his relationships within that group. One student's bearing bore a marked relationship to the progress of his emotional attitude to one of the female members of the student group. Hence, an individual student's bearing depended just as much on the tutor/organiser's ability to manage the group relationships as upon a particular tutor's ability to teach a skill.

Confidence as a 'feeling of being at ease within oneself'

Some students were unsure of the meaning of the word 'confidence' in its most basic sense and the phrase 'feeling more at ease within yourself' was offered to them for comment. Clumsy though it was, the phrase seemed to describe the students' perception; though they selected several levels of such inner ease. One student thought of it in terms of his skill performance:

> And I feel *easier in my own mind.* I can now work out all the big words by working it out in the sentence. So that I know what it is now.

Another student saw the phrase through his social activities:

Interviewer: We met two years ago. Looking back, has it been worth it?

Student: Oh, yes, definitely. The lessons I had were definitely worth it. I am a lot more confident now. . . . Yes, much more confidence. I am now doing things that I would not have attempted to do before. I go along to help at my son's club during the evenings.

One student replies to the question by first describing his work in minute detail, the point being that he had to make notes of the performance of his machine. He continued:

> Oh – confidence: yes, confidence in my own ability really. A bit of skill in reading and writing. The most valuable (thing) is that I have not to rely on somebody else. It is my own confidence that I can struggle and *get by*. I will not say perfect. But I can get along without having to run off to somebody to put me right. I try and get by on my own now. Before I used to have to ask somebody.

Yet another student realised the implication of the question and his basic attitude:

Interviewer: Do you feel easier in yourself?

Student: Oh, yes. You (I) feel much easier when I go out and about. . . .

Interviewer: Do you think the ease within yourself is as important as the skill of reading and writing?

Student: Yes, that is important, very important, because if you get easier in your mind then you can do things. When you go out with others, you can still do *part* of it (reading and writing). And you *do not feel as though you have to stand in the background all the time.*

The recognition of the importance of this achievement of helping students to feel 'more at ease within themselves' was far more explicit in the second interviews with tutors. A tutor who most clearly thought of herself as teaching reading and writing to adults, in the first interview, reassessed the priorities in the second interview:

Tutor: His confidence has improved. I have at times said to him that I feel that what I can teach him is going to be very limited and there is very little more that I can teach him. This is because the *same old* spelling mistakes are made time after time and he does not remember the rules. Then he told me that the greatest thing in his week was coming here. . . . He writes screeds about things with *countless* mistakes. . . .

Interviewer: Have your ideas about teaching adult literacy changed?

Tutor: Yes, I feel that it is a very, very complicated business. It is becoming more so and I think it is a much slower process than I ever thought it.

After that conversation the student was interviewed in his tutor's presence and as the student's real gratitude for 'ease within my mind' emerged, the tutor's optimism seemed to return. At the end of the session she remarked: 'Well, I suppose I'm not doing a bad job after all, but it's not only the reading and writing, is it? There is more to it, and I think it's worth it!'

Thus, from all the tutors, though more so from those teaching in their homes, the stated recognition of the primacy of 'feeling at ease within myself' as a constituent of confidence only emerged strongly in the second interviews, and the importance of 'confidence' overall increased. As these criteria were recognised, so the 'training' as distinct from the 'education' element in the total adult education process tended to diminish in importance and the skills occupied a place lower down the scale of criteria.

Confidence to make personal reassessments

In a curious way the students seemed to recognise both the importance of building up their confidence and also the fact that their improvement in skills would be a time-consuming process in which only *small advances* would be made. A typical response is that of the student who, asked 'If I were to take on a new student myself and I told him that this was an easy six-week job, what would you say?' replied:

> No, no, it is *not*! It's very difficult – it's very, very difficult to bring yourself. You learn things as you go through life and you take on responsibilities. You can do all those things. When it comes to this, it is a very difficult thing to put yourself in somebody's hands and say to yourself, 'You are going back to school again.' To go back to being someone of nine years old is a very hard thing to do. You have to bring yourself down the scale again.

Thus, the average illiterate who persisted, and did not give up as soon as he had gone beyond the stage of catching up to the level of skill which he had attained at school, *was prepared to reconsider his personal attitudes*, particularly to the problem of learning as an adult. The best example of this came from one of two students who said that they now lost their temper with people less frequently:

> I have a fairly quick temper and I say what I think when I should not do so. I do not do that as often as I used to do. I think now. It has something to do with reading. I am sure it has something

to do with it. Even when I should fly off the handle, with good reason, I do not. Yes, *I think I am more confident in me.* (You feel this is an inner confidence?) Yes, yes!

The tutor of the other student, who admitted to having lost his temper frequently before starting his course, remarked:

He has really come out of himself. He is so normal, amiable and easy to be with . . . but then he has been here for several years.

Confidence to weigh evidence

Sometimes the students' ability to assess evidence for themselves increased, and this indicated some increase of self-confidence.

Well, there is always certain things in the paper that is not on the news. Yes, I notice them. I read about Ali's fight and I thought it was a good scrap – in the newspaper! But on the telly, he got knocked down four times!

Confidence to evangelise

Another sign of a change in confidence is perhaps the *willingness to evangelise.* A few students were extremely active in this and they were the ones who stated that they felt considerably more confident. Typical of those who did try to spread the good news is the rather vivid evidence of the student who said:

Yes, I have. There is a drinking pal of mine of about 40 years old. I have tried to get him to come in. He cannot even write his name. I can do that. But he cannot and he will not come. He is in the same boat I was. He does not care who knows that he cannot read but he will not come to the sessions. Yes, I have told him. I have even got a poster up in my window. *I would not have done that before.*

Confidence to be self-reliant

The next major criterion exemplifying an increase in confidence was the growth of the students' fundamental self-reliance, e.g.:

> I have more confidence in writing reports which I have to do frequently.

and:

> It helps me shopping, reading the stuff that we wanted, food and going to buy records. Once upon a time I could not read them (the record labels) and I used to get a young girl aged eight to come to . . . to choose them with me. She used to come and read all the records for me to choose.

and even more conclusively:

> Well, they do not look at you the way that you have got to ask them all the time. Sort of thing! You can do it yourself. (Independence?) Independence, yes, if you want to know!

> There is definitely a feeling of independence – definitely, it is a change – independence, that's right!

And, as an example of the happiness that flows from that feeling of emerging self-reliance:

> Confidence? That has increased, definitely! Funny that you should ask that because my husband has just been getting over flu and has been in bed. One or two bills needed to be done. I did these and wrote the cheques for them quite happily. And *he* was very happy! Oh, yes! He is a great help to me because he says, 'Well, you do it then. It is practice for you!'

Confidence as evidenced by self-assurance

Similarly, self-assurance may be listed as a further criterion of progress in confidence, e.g.:

> Achievement? I would like to think so. Well, you need not take my word for it but the girl friend has recognised that . . . well . . . I have a lot more self-assurance. I feel that I am at last doing something definite about it.

> Sometimes I take over. (Leadership of a voluntary group.) I find that I can go now and say, 'Well, no; I do not think that that is right.' Before I would just sit because I would be sort of worried

about saying the wrong words. Being able to write them down and having to do it ... doing the work, I find that I can talk to people better as well. It helps me both ways ... I do get carried away a bit!

It is, of course, difficult to prove but one senses that as the student's self-assurance grows, the truer nature of the individual may be revealed and appreciated; and that the student, intuitively aware of this reappraisal, responds further. One student, who looked like an all-in wrestler and could be extremely tough, was pretty formidable in the first interview. As one began to know him better over the course of two years, one began to understand the inner worth of the man and the limitations of single-interview research techniques. The tutor's evidence not only describes his growth in terms of self-assurance but delineates, unconsciously, the characteristics of a good tutor:

When I first came he was waiting for you to write every word and he would then laboriously copy it. So, yes, in three years he has altered by that amount. A lot of effort goes into what appears to be little achievement in the skills. Yet to that individual it is a great step forward. But this is it; *I expect him* to suddenly make another breakthrough. The one so far this term is that he has started to spell on his own. That has been a tremendous break-through and I am delighted by it. He is *really* working class – (pause) – but *such* a gentleman with it.

The answers to the questions put to the student referred to above were crisp, direct and to the point:

Interviewer: So your last year has not been a waste of time?

Student: Not whatsoever. No. *And you know that!*

Interviewer: Tailed off?

Student: No, steady progress all the time.

Interviewer: Easier with people?

Student: Definitely!

Interviewer: With your family?

Student: Definitely!

Confidence as evidenced by a diminution in anxiety

If 'confidence' has improved, students should have experienced some diminution in anxiety, in a general sense. In practice, most tutors and students referred to 'embarrassment' as the description of a lack of confidence. As time passed it became clear that many students and tutors had seen at least one, though never all, of the programmes of a BBC series called 'On the Move'. Indeed, nearly half the students interviewed had been invited to a pilot programme at their adult education centre. These programmes included accounts by selected adult illiterates, who usually explained their disadvantage by the word 'embarrassment'. Consequently it became a catchword and, for this reason, some students were provided with a scale of words, to help them to identify various levels of anxiety. These were, in descending order of anxiety:

panic
dread
alarm
trepidation
embarrassment
disquiet
apprehension
unease
defeatism
self-distrust
depression
defensiveness
qualms.

Most students asked what each word meant when the list was read out to them; many students looked at the list as it was read to them and pointed to the word, or rather to the *position* of the word, which they thought best described their feelings. The interesting point to emerge was that the words chosen by the students were at the top extreme of the scale, whereas tutors used the whole range. It seems that no matter how empathetic the tutor is, it is nearly impossible to reach into the feelings of a student who has experienced difficulty in a common mode of human communication.

This is not a criticism of tutors. A tutor who admits, quite cheerfully, to making spelling mistakes herself may perceive a student, whose lack of skill is a matter of poor spelling, as being in a state of defensiveness. Yet when the student is asked about his own perception, the replies are usually of the following kind:

I have been conscious of this all my life . . . it is a *continual* worry.

. . . feelings of *horror* . . . it is unfortunate that I was made to feel I had a stigma!

. . . *dread* at being found out!

Well, I am really in a state of *panic*. I do not like people knowing. Well, not many know really. Only just my family. It is between dread and panic.

I would not like anybody to know. I feel about *trepidation*; a little more than embarrassment. I feel that people tend to look down on you. I mean, we cannot help it! They look down on you!

There is also the comment of the student who felt that the interviewer was perhaps complacent and patronising:

You do not know what it means to have this problem. How can you? You can do it? So don't * * * * come it, mate!

Thus, the use of *one* word 'embarrassment' to describe the feelings of students is clearly inadequate, and one of the signs of an increase in confidence seems to be that the student sees himself over a period of time as descending the scale of anxiety.

Checks to the growth of confidence

So far, the more successful students have been considered. In fact, there are students who lose confidence. Some of those who gave up after a very few weeks may have screwed up enough courage and confidence to come forward and then found their confidence ebbing. Sometimes it could be due to over-expectations on the part of the tutor:

Student (1976): She is going a little bit too fast for me – she thinks I am better than I am.

Tutor (1977): She has not contacted me since I last saw you (1976).

Sometimes loss of confidence was due to extraneous circumstances well beyond the control of the tutor, such as an unsympathetic employer, a jealous wife:

Since I started, she reads large fat books, when she is washing-up, all the time!

97

Sometimes the very friendliness of an adult centre made the evenings between seem very lonely:

> I was coming to classes before this (court) case came up, but the classes kept me going because I do not have anybody to talk to. *You* do not look out of it like that, do you?

Sometimes relationships in one-to-one tuition at home went awry; the friendliness of the smart young housewife was misinterpreted and the impression on the rejected student could hardly have increased his confidence.

Similarly, over-friendliness between tutor and student could result in a lack of progress in skills and, as has been noted, the relationship between skills and confidence is a two-way one.

Inevitably then, the failure in skills must to some degree inhibit growth of confidence, particularly if the tutor does not appreciate that provision of companionship and friendliness might be the most potent educational force that can be applied in some specific circumstances. One tutor reported with some disappointment that:

> Well, I think she could go further but she just did not put in enough time, quite honestly. Really and truly, unless you are going to work at it every week, you are not going to do much anyway. We found that after every gap we had to start again. So I do not have her any more. It was very sad; I had to sit and wait and she did not turn up. I would not get an apology or perhaps she would phone the next day. I think this is perhaps because we became friendly. I think that, in future, it is better to keep it as a strictly business arrangement. You know I think perhaps if it becomes too friendly you are taken advantage of, you know. I thought it would perhaps work out. *Anyway she learned an awful lot in the time.*

Furthermore, it was clear that progress in 'confidence' could be limited in certain situations. For example, some students never wrote a thing except in the presence of their tutor. Their confidence was limited to the ambience of their tutor/student relationship. A tutor reported that:

> He is working (in his job) with a man who knows that he cannot read and keeps rubbing it in, which has made him more tense than ever ... I can see it ... his home life, he thinks, has improved.

Here the student had gained in confidence sufficiently to feel that home relationships had improved but the increase was not enough to deal with a less sympathetic person at his place of work.

Confidence, subcultures and functional literacy

We have shown that the lack of confidence can be a limiting factor in the acquisition and utilisation of skills. It is also discernible that a lack of confidence may lead to the lack of use of a particular skill and it is difficult to forecast, in practice, precisely how the student will respond to the knowledge he has gained from his studies. To place this behaviour in a generalised pattern the ethological approach is the most appropriate, for each student has his own subculture, either chosen or imposed, in which he must survive. Consequently, so far as the student is concerned, whatever the skill, it has no significance for him unless it is used 'functionally'. But the term 'functional' has a peculiar and particular meaning which is ethological rather than sociological: in this context, 'functional' means a response to a subcultural environment which the student thinks will increase his viability within that environment. The following conversation with a particular student, her tutor and her husband, demonstrates this point:

Interviewer: How about reading?

Student: The reading is marvellous. . . .

Tutor: Yet we did not really do a great deal of reading. We concentrated on spelling!

Interviewer: Well, how about writing?

Student: I still intend to continue and I still do three or four pages *over again* to do one page. When I write one letter (for practice) then I go through that book (dictionary) and correct my own spelling. *I am still not sure in my mind about the spelling. I have not got that confidence.*

Husband: There was a time when she would not do it (anything to do with reading) at all. She is reading a lot more in the last two years, probably more than ever before. . . .

Student: We meet every Wednesday; we did a course in home nursing; lift people, make a bed and so on. *That was marvellous because I did not have to write – I did not have to spell anything.*

Interviewer: Have you written an actual letter to anybody?

Student: No, there again, the phone . . . I can just pick it up. It is an easy way out to me.

Interviewer: Looking back, how would you put, in order of importance, writing, reading or confidence?

Student: I think confidence more than anything else. (Very much so?) Yes, I think so. Next comes the reading. *I find that useful and I use it.*

Thus, to take a particular case, this student who spent most of her time learning to write, in fact used reading as the functional response to an environment which provided a telephone and which required largely, if not solely, the technical ability to read. Because she was not continuously challenged about her writing, her survival, in terms of human relationships, was not at risk. Two points emerge from the above quotation, that:

(a) the tutor's subculture differs from that of the student and both individuals perceive in terms of their own subcultures, and

(b) the student is confident in general, but not over spelling for which there is no immediate environmental demand.

Teachers and sociologists regard spelling as one of the proper demands of society as a whole and it is these demands which determine their definition of functional literacy. On the other hand, the students' first, and possibly only, demand for literacy is in terms of their own particular subculture. The evidence suggests that any attempt to persuade a student to meet the demands of *society as a whole* must follow *after confidence has been established*, enabling him to break out of his subculture, if he so wishes.

Summary

Whether a student acquired confidence or not depended on the warmth of the tutor's personality; her knowledge of the aims of adult education, whether acquired through training schemes or by instinctive empathy; on the relationship of the student with the tutor and, quite often, with other students; and on extraneous factors to do with the ordinary process of survival. Confidence was rarely a simple entity and usually the students who gained generally in confidence would display a lack of it in particular activities or perceptions not required in the first instance by his subculture.

Thus, confidence may be defined as being composed of:

(a) an improvement in bearing (physical attribute)

(b) a feeling of ease within oneself

(c)   a willingness to reconsider personal attitudes
(d)   an ability to assess evidence
(e)   a willingness to evangelise
(f)   an improvement in self-reliance
(g)   an improvement in assurance
(h)   a diminution in anxiety

and: increases in confidence associated with literacy skills (see Chapter X).

Although the notion of confidence is complex, it is the basic constituent of affective personal achievement and because of its importance, it places affective personal achievement as the prime, yet pervasive, objective of a project concerned with ameliorating adult illiteracy or, indeed, of any project concerned with subcultures of the 'disadvantaged'.

VI Cognitive achievements

1 Reading skills

Because of the emphasis of most training schemes and from their own experience of teaching children, tutors thought of the skills of reading and the objectives of their teaching in terms of such taxonomies as the Barrett taxonomy.* This taxonomy of criteria lists five major accomplishments:

1 *literal comprehension*, including recognition and recall;
2 *reorganisation skills*, including classifying, summarising and synthesising;
3 *inferential comprehension*, including inferring details, ideas, sequence and relationships;
4 *evaluation skills*, including judgements of reality, opinion, validity and appropriateness;
5 *appreciation skills*, including such emotional responses as appreciation of character development and language imagery as presented by the author.

Many tutors began by expecting their students gradually to develop all these skills, but after a short period of time those that did not give up accepted that:

(i)   their students' aims were different, in that most individual students had objectives which were specific to his/her own requirements;
(ii) progress would be limited;

* For a detailed list of Barrett's taxonomy, see Appendix 0, p. 158, in *Developing Fluent Reading*, Open University Course Book PE 231, Block Units 1, 2, 3 and 4, by John Chapman and Mary Hoffman; Open University, Milton Keynes, UK, 1977.

(iii) there could be gaps in a student's skill displaying a very low ability even to recognise some words and that this could be associated with an ease of recognition of more difficult words.

The following quotations illustrate these points.

(i) *Acceptance of the student's objective as the criterion of reading success*
He can read though sometimes he has to work it out. He is a bit on the slow side but he does read a newspaper for himself and he reads with his children which I think was one of the objectives of the exercise . . . he is obviously fond of his children . . . I do not think he has a lot of outside interests.

(ii) *Acceptance of limited progress in reading*
That is one of the things that made me *rethink* slightly. The people that I was teaching would never be reading the greats – the things that I would read . . . but even to get them to read a newspaper and to take an interest in political things – to be aware – things like that.

(iii) *Recognition of more difficult words and inconsistent progress*
Student: Don't know that word!
Tutor: What is the first meal of the day?
Student: Breakfast!

Tutor's evidence continued:

So often she will get the word 'elephant' right . . . usually with long words, they seem to get hold of them far easier than the short words; 'then' becomes 'they'. Little words seem to confuse them.

Consequently when tutors in the research sample were asked to assess their students' progress in reading the questions were framed to take account of their perceptions of the students' aims in coming forward for tuition in reading, and six criteria of progress were established:

1 increase in word recognition skills
2 increase in sentence recognition skills
3 increase in comprehension skills
4 increase in the ability to read informational texts
5 increase in the ability to read texts beyond the purely informational levels
6 increase in the ability to read newspapers.

Throughout this study it has been emphasised that there was a complete spectrum of cognitive ability, ranging from the student who could hardly read a word to the student who could read simple versions of Jane Austen's works. Thus, progress in individual students was measured from several base levels but, nevertheless, the outstanding feature that emerged from this study was that, proportionately, progress in reading in general terms came second to that in confidence gains. The quotations illustrating progress in reading, by each of the six criteria given above, clearly exemplify the general feeling of both tutors and students that success in this area of skills was noteworthy and satisfactory.

1 *Increase in word recognition*

Very *few* students could not read the common social words, or, rather, recognise them. 'Men' or 'Gentlemen' were words recognised as being different from 'Ladies'; similarly 'left turn' looked different to 'right turn'. Since, in functional contexts, most of these words were supported by signs, very few students had difficulty in coping practically with such examples. Nevertheless, there were examples of students with very basic reading skills and the speech of these students was usually so heavily accented that:

> Her knowledge has obviously not been based on phonetics and sounds of words, so maybe she can do harder words and then stops at a *simple* one. She is erratic. She reads, it is the basic stuff she does not know.

> He can read reasonably well, but if you give him a word like *bat* or *mat* and say 'Make another word out of that by changing the first letter' he will look at you and say 'What?'

But of this student, the tutor/organiser was able to say that *after a period of attendance of some three years*, the student:

> . . . has slightly improved since you saw him 18 months ago — more than slightly. He went at a tremendous pace for a certain time and then seemed to reach his peak and I feel that he has been on a plateau for a length of time. At that point, I felt that he was really making no progress but I think he will go on again because he is still quite keen to work hard at it.

And the student's view of the matter?

Student: Getting on very well!

Interviewer: Is your reading getting better?

Student: Yes.

2 Increase in sentence recognition skills

The great majority of students who came to learn to read wished to acquire sufficient skill to read sentences, paragraphs or whole texts. Most of these, of course, had to be helped with particular words, but their main problem was that of anticipation and prediction. Their progress was largely in terms of sentence recognition skills, because most of them did not, in fact, read any text continuously but rather attacked a paragraph at a time. As one student described his reading:

> Steady progress (overall), not rapid. Reading has increased quite considerably. Now I will push myself to read something; an odd notice or something that comes through the door. I will attempt to read it.

The impression was that he would read enough to make sense of the text, and that probably he would decode only a few sentences at a time. This was as far as most students wished to go, for if they had learnt that much they could read any information that was absolutely necessary (e.g. the Highway Code) and they could get the gist of a newspaper's heavy print story which immediately follows the headline.

In a few cases tutors were bitterly disappointed that their students went no further because, in principle, to read sentences is to be able to read books. One such tutor said:

> I say there is nothing wrong with his intelligence but he is not using his skill. Children at school do not just have three or five reading lessons a week; they pick up books to do arithmetic, geography or anything, and you see *he is not reading!*

However, the great majority of tutors and students in the sample were delighted to have reached this stage, but then about 50 per cent of the students were already there before they joined the scheme anyway. Only about half of all the students wanted reading practice and these were given help in the comprehension skills.

3 Increase in comprehension skills

The main feature of these skills is to understand the burden of the argument in the text. For example, as a tutor reported:

> Very good at reading, yes, very good. He definitely *understands*

what he is reading now. He is reading books for the first time.

and the student perceived his progress as:

> Yes, you know, it (the lessons) helped me a lot with the reading; once you learn how to pronounce a word *you get along* with the reading. I have read *The Journey to the Centre of the Earth* by Jules Verne right the way through. That is the first time I have read for a long time (period). Each time I used to get fed up and pack it up. No, I could not do it two years ago. No. That is the biggest thing that I have managed.

or:

> But if he has a straightforward book he *understands* what he reads and he is interested in reading. Whether he will ever become a great reader I do not know.

and, as an implicit example of increased skill in comprehension:

> Oh, he is improving. He has an impediment in his speech but I still think his reading is better than it used to be (i.e. testing his reading was difficult because of the speech impediment). He is reading library books; he has now a *habit* of borrowing books from the library and he reads full-length books quite easily. I do not think he read quite so much before. I think he was able to read newspapers before.

But there were some students who had started at a lower level of skill and who had just begun to understand what they were reading. One such, a fairly typical case, was described as follows:

Tutor: Well it is very difficult to know what to say in answer to your question 'Any progress in reading?' He has just continued very slow but very steady progress. He has gone on to a better type of book now. He is reading a bowdlerised version of Ian Fleming's *Dr No*. Really, on the whole he seems to be getting on quite well with it. He gets occasionally stumped over the odd word but, on the whole, he gets on quite well. I have some reservations about the level of comprehension but I think he has continued to make slow but noticeable progress.

Interviewer: Would he have been capable of reading *Dr No* when he came to you?

Tutor: No, I would not think so. No, he could not even read paragraphs out of the local paper on subjects which were of particular interest to him. I should think, no, certainly not! It is being read, of course, *in conventional novel print.* When he started I had him on the Adventure Reading Series with print three times the normal size. Incidentally, he has got another of Ian Fleming's books, in the same style, the simplified version, at home and he is reading that to his wife. Apparently he is enjoying the story very much. Now I have *never ever* had him read anything before and say that *he was actually interested in the plot.*

As well as the general increase in the students' ability to exercise the comprehension skills, tutors reported increments in reading skills in terms of very definite task achievements, such as reading the Highway Code (an informational text), reading poetry or reading a newspaper. Indeed, one experienced tutor argued that:

> I try to pin down my pupils to realistic aims right from the beginning. As soon as I see them I say, 'Let's write a list of the exact things that we are aiming at, so that we can tick them off when we do them.' I am sorry I have not got any of these lists for you to see because we destroy all papers about students as soon as we have finished with the students, for reasons of confidentiality. However, they would include such things as wanting to write a cheque, notices, minutes for a meeting and so on.

Interviewer: So most students come with a specific literacy aim?

Tutor: Most of the *intelligent* ones and the ones *who find it easier to learn* certainly have specific aims.

Based on such evidence, often repeated in other versions, the remaining three major criteria of success in reading were extracted.

4 *Increase in ability to read informational texts*
Informational texts are written in differing styles demanding different levels of ability, and students often specify the need to read certain pamphlets as their objectives. The higher the level of skill which the student had already attained, the higher the level of informational pamphlet that he usually wished to be able to read; thus, students generally acted as self-selectors and often gave an example of a type of informational pamphlet within their possible level of achievement. It must be stressed that other informational pamphlets were brought to their tutor for explanation and completion, in much the same way

as highly literate people take their income tax demand form with its accompanying information leaflet to their accountant. Examples of the type of pamphlets which students regarded as criteria of personal reading success were:

> I can fill in my car form by myself and the licence form. I can do those by myself. *That* makes a big difference.

> I will read the odd notice that comes through the door – advertising material. Before I used to just put it aside or leave it for the wife or something like that!

> I plumbed the kitchen sink unit and there was no trouble because I could look up my Do-It-Yourself instruction manual.

> Helps me with DIY instructions, definitely!

> I can do time sheets at work (read headings and complete).

> I can read words on the telly now and again, if they stay on for a few seconds.

5   *Increase in ability to read texts beyond purely informational levels*
Progress in this ability is relative to the student's starting level of reading skill, although in fact the actual reading levels of the students who had declared themselves in need of general literacy work was quite startling; many students could read perfectly well:

> Reading? That was all right! That was not the trouble!

Other students refurbished their reading capability whilst taking lessons in writing; for example, there was the student who had writing lessons only but who thought that her tutor was responsible for the improvement in her reading ability. Of her reading she said:

> The reading is marvellous. I can read anything. I do not gallop along. I used to pick something up and just gallop! Now I stop and watch the words.

Tutor: She used to jump at things and make up her mind about something instead of reading it carefully.

Student: Yes, now I sort of stop, and I break the words up *as if I am writing them.* Another book I have been reading is Bellamy's – that is a marvellous book. His words are long sometimes. But what I do is to break them down. The names of flowers you know! I could not even pronounce them. I sit there and make three or four words and join them up all together! What I like is that I can pick up a book and READ!

Some students read books to their children, usually of the simple, short-story variety, but their descriptions of their pleasure in reading aloud – with meaning and emphasis – were heartwarming. Other students read poetry books for the first time in their lives, and yet others read the book of a television series, such as 'Poldark', and compared the written version to the visual version.

Many students, often those who said they could read before joining the scheme, registered a new sense of pleasure, of sheer enjoyment, at being able to read books. Tutors recognised, therefore, that one of their major criteria for success was the willingness and ability to read a continuous text, and reading *a book* beyond an informational level was an important milestone which, though far short of *War and Peace* was, nevertheless, a marker in the way to self-awareness.

> There was another book about the first airmen or something – he took that home for Christmas!

> She would take responsibility if she wanted. It did not show you this – on the telly. You know, I was *rather glad* I had read the book. It was completely different!

> I just want to get up and read my favourite hymn!

> You know, she *enjoyed* reading a book. She read quite a bit really. She could read with understanding.

6 *Increase in ability to read newspapers*

A further mark of progress was the ability and willingness to read a newspaper. Various levels of reading skill are required between newspapers, and even within the same newspaper. Most students read the simpler tabloids and many students only read the headlines or large-print paragraphs or particular pages. Nevertheless, typically, tutors and students frequently mentioned newspaper reading:

> My student is now taking a newspaper to work (*The Sun*), writing Christmas cards and reading the literacy project magazine. . . .

> Oh, yes. Reading newspapers! He always bought newspapers, so he told me, but now he buys newspapers *and he reads them*!

> Well, I can read a newspaper right the way through. Two years ago – no! I used to read some of it and then pack it up. I can read the papers I am supposed to read instead of making believe that I could do!

> Newspapers now. I used to read bits two years ago and then it turned out that these were the *main* bits!

But not all students reach that level easily; for example:

Newspapers? Well, yes and no, really! Say something comes up like the advertisement I saw the other night, that I did not know or I was not quite sure of or I could not break it down. Then I usually get the missus to read it. And all of a sudden I say, 'Oh, yes! That's quite right. Yes, I should have known that!' But there are some words I still miss.

It was extremely interesting to hear tutors who had emphasised the criteria of reading success in quite high-level technical jargon during the first series of interviews switch to the criteria suggested above during the second series of interviews. One particular tutor spoke of 'dyslexia, tests, eye-tests' and of finding that he was 'acutely cross-lateral' and that 'he did not sequence properly' and of taking 'reading age tests'. At that time the tutor reported that:

We are reading the 'Mrs. Pepperpot' omnibus which has a reasonable size of script; he can read 'caught' and 'thought' in context. . . . In fact he reads quite difficult words like 'brightness' which he manages quite readily. He, curiously enough, like so many people like this, gets caught out on words that you really would not expect. He continually falls down on 'what' and reads it as 'that' . . . *candidly, my personal view is that I have not* made much progress with him.

Yet about 15 months later the same student was reading an Ian Fleming book to his wife, and in answer to the question 'What has he achieved?' the tutor replied:

No. 1 – confidence, as, for example, his jury service.
No. 2 – reading skills.
No. 3 – writing skills.
He does not have to use his writing at all at work except in so far as he fills in a licence application. The writing skill area is definitely the field in which he has made *least* progress!

Indeed, this tutor's evidence was typical; most students could decode far better than they could encode, probably because they were required more often to do so and thereby they had practice in decoding. In their ordinary lives they would read signs, the television programme schedules, knitting patterns, newspapers or novelettes; these would all be read slowly and painstakingly by some, quicker by others, but read nevertheless.

So far as reading was concerned, embarrassment occurred when they had to read aloud and in public. Consequently they would prefer to take home something to read slowly in their own time or to read with the help of their spouse. Often, once a document was read there was no need to reply other than orally. Thus, for example, a poor reader would be able to read the rate or rent demand from the local authority; if he disagreed he would go along to the council office and argue the case, or use the telephone.

Though decoding was usually practised by students from the day they left school, encoding certainly was not. Moreover, encoding required organisation, the assembly of ideas in a logical order, and this was exactly the characteristic so markedly missing in the vast majority of students. Some could run successful businesses, run successful lives, but that is not the same as writing successfully; there is no necessary transfer of abilities from other fields to writing and it was one of the features of the literacy campaign that this simple proposition was ignored. Hence the surprise of both tutors and students that progress in writing was usually both slow and limited.

Many tutors who had helped their students to revise, and had brought their students up to the level that they had attained at school thought, in the early months of the campaign in 1975-6, that real, large-scale, speedy progress would be made. By mid-1977 there was universal acceptance of the realities of the encoding problem. It was the writing problem that caused a tutor to comment (and many other tutors to hint):

> It is a very, very complicated business . . . it is a much slower process than I ever thought it was . . . we have had 54 sessions of about one-and-a-half hours . . . but he is *not* using his writing – he does not have to.

Since, by mid-1977, some tutors were remarking that the campaign should have been called the 'Adult Reading Campaign', not the 'Adult Literacy Campaign', and because of the general agreement of students and tutors that writing, in all its aspects, improved least, the next section dealing with the criteria for achievement in writing starts with a description of an investigation of progress in writing skills based on the actual work of students as judged by independent panels.

2 Writing skills

To assess the improvement or otherwise in the written work of the students, students were asked to provide samples of what they considered to be their best work, with an average interval of six months between each piece of work. Twenty-seven students agreed to co-operate and panels of assessors were chosen to evaluate their work.

Panel A consisted of 13 practising teachers, with experience in either primary, secondary or specialist remedial education, who were attending a part-time course at an institute of education; Panel B comprised six more experienced teachers who were attending a full-time English course at the same institute of education, together with two experts in the teaching of literacy.

Panel A was asked to assess whether, compared with their experience of children's work, the first piece of each adult's written work was similar to that of a child aged between five up to eight years, eight up to 13 years, or 13 up to 16 years. Then Panel A evaluated each adult's second piece of work in the same way. Altogether the teachers made 329 individual judgements of each of the two sets of adult work.

This panel thought that the first piece of the students' written work indicated that, out of 329 scripts:

207 were equivalent to a child aged five up to eight years (62.92 per cent)

111 were equivalent to a child aged eight up to 13 years (33.74 per cent)

11 were equivalent to a child aged 13 up to 16 years (3.34 per cent).

The second piece of work, which had been completed about six months later, was assessed as showing that, out of 329 scripts:

166 were equivalent to a child aged five up to eight years (50.46 per cent)

140 were equivalent to a child aged eight up to 13 years (42.55 per cent)

23 were equivalent to a child aged 13 up to 16 years (6.99 per cent).

No attempt was made to analyse whether a *particular* student had moved from one group to another, since the assumption in using panels of adjudicators is that aggregate decisions are likely to be correct even though single judgements may be highly individual.

In view of the rough three-part division into child-equivalent ages, it seemed prudent to use this part of the questionnaire solely as an indicator. Nonetheless, the generally low level of attainment is shown by the fact that, of the *total of 658* assessments, only 34 were placed in the eldest child-equivalent group of 13 up to 16 years.

Secondly, the members of Panel A were asked to judge whether the work of each of the students, taken in chronological order, was 'worse', 'about the same' or had 'improved' in the following seven ways:

(a) handwriting (motor skills)
(b) spelling (in terms of spelling precedent in English)
(c) use of words of more than *two* syllables
(d) sentence length
(e) level of communication
(f) punctuation
(g) attack.

Twelve panel members (one form was rejected) made 304 judgements
in each of the seven categories, with the following results:

Category	Percentage 'worse'
spelling	2
use of words	3
punctuation	3
sentence length	5
level of communication	5
attack	5
handwriting	8

Category	Percentage 'about the same'
handwriting	41
level of communication	43
attack	46
sentence length	48
spelling	56
punctuation	56
use of words	59

Category	Percentage 'improved'
use of words	38
punctuation	41
spelling	42
sentence length	47
attack	49
handwriting	51
level of communication	52

Thus the responses of the panel to the second part of the questionnaire
indicated that between:

2 per cent and 8 per cent were *worse* in some respect,

41 per cent and 59 per cent were *about the same* in some respect, and 38 per cent and 52 per cent had *improved* in some respect.

During the discussion that followed the adjudication process, the members of Panel A indicated that they had experienced great difficulty in recalling the writing age of an average child in each age group; they said that it depended largely on their experience of the average standard in their particular school which itself, in turn, depended on the catchment area of that school and the ability and willingness of parents to encourage their children *to practise* their writing. Therefore, in the opinion of Panel A, the acceptable standard of, say, a five-year-old child in one area differed markedly from that in another area. This raises fascinating questions about conceptions of national standards which are outside the scope of this study. Nevertheless, the evidence of these teachers provides yet a further case for rejecting reading ages as a criterion of progress for adults and for adopting the methodology advanced in this book.

Panel B was asked to complete only the second part of the form, i.e. the seven categories section. The six experienced teachers worked as three pairs, so that each pair could make an assessment after discussion, whilst the two experts in the teaching of literacy judged individually; thus five forms were completed. The conclusions of Panel B were as follows:

Category	*Percentage 'worse'*
spelling	5
use of words	5
sentence length	7
attack	8
level of communication	9
punctuation	9
handwriting	14

Category	*Percentage 'about the same'*
level of communication	24
handwriting	27
attack	27
use of words	28
sentence length	33
spelling	45
punctuation	46

Category	Percentage 'improved'
punctuation	45
spelling	50
handwriting	59
sentence length	60
attack	65
use of words	67
level of communication	67

The responses of Panel B suggested, therefore, that between:

5 per cent and 14 per cent were *worse* in some respect,
24 per cent and 46 per cent were *about the same* in some respect, and
45 per cent and 67 per cent had *improved* in some respect.

Two points emerged from the discussion that followed the completion of the form:

(a) the judgements of Panel B agreed with the outline of the assessment given by the students' tutors of the progress in writing of *particular* students as recorded on the tapes, and

(b) Panel B had a more uniform, sophisticated and precise idea of the criteria on which to judge each of the seven categories; in discussion they defined them as follows:

Category	Criteria
Handwriting	Skill, control, whether cursive or not, care, legibility or formation and uniformity over the whole script.
Spelling	The difficulty of the words used together with allowances for their nearness to phonic usage.
Words of more than two syllables	The impression of the frequency of such words in each of the two sample pieces of the student's work.
Sentence length	The impression of the length of sentences in each of the two sample pieces of the student's work.
Level of communication	The ability to express ideas and to organise thought.
Punctuation	The impression of use and the degree of usage.
Attack	The purposiveness of the written work.

Consequently the 'opinions' of Panel B were taken to be probably more reliable but, nevertheless, broad conclusions were drawn by reference to the 'opinions' of *both* panels, particularly where there was an overall measure of agreement. Accordingly:

(a)   the range of improvement was probably between 45 per cent and 67 per cent over all categories;

(b)   the range of 'worse' performance was in the overall range of 5 per cent to 14 per cent;

(c)   proportionately *fewer* students *were worse* in spelling;

(d)   proportionately *more* students *were worse* in handwriting;

(e)   about *half* the students were the *same* in both spelling and handwriting;

(f)   *over half* improved in handwriting *but*

(g)   the *greatest range of performance* was in handwriting;

(h)   the *greatest proportional improvement* was in the level of communication.

Thus, in the 'opinions' of the panels, the students' handwriting altered most of all the writing skills, and most students seemed to increase in *confidence* sufficiently to attempt to communicate at a higher level. From the discussions, it became clear that both panels were surprised at the low level of writing skill as evidenced in *both* the pieces of work provided by each student.

As in the case of reading, although many tutors started with rather complicated ideas of the techniques of writing, the objectives in this particular skill became fairly simple and basic. Seven categories emerged from the evidence:

1   improvement in the motor skill of writing
2   improvement in spelling
3   improvement in the ability to check spelling
4   improvement in the ability to take dictation
5   an ability to complete commonly-used forms or questionnaires
6   improvement in the ability to write letters
7   improvement in the ability to write extended prose texts.

In judging the performance of individual students, improvements or achievements depended on the starting base level of each student, but although there was a range of ability equal to that noted in reading, the spread of ability was generally at a far lower level. The following is an exceptional case:

He came in his late twenties with what he thought was an enormous writing and spelling problem. It just dissolved. It just went. I found that I was having to prepare a tremendous amount of work each week; he just took off; he did not know how good he was.

But the more usual case was that of the student who:

> ... was a very poor speller – she had no idea – she did not really know that 70 per cent of the language was regular (I think it is 70 per cent!). She did not realise that there was a pattern to things, generally speaking. I think she mastered a few words, such as 'apple' ends with an 'l' followed by an 'e' and not an 'e' followed by an 'l'.

At the other end of the spectrum were a few students, usually with the background of special schooling for the educationally subnormal, whose accomplishment would be no more than to write a few common words legibly. These students, like all the rest, were much better at reading than writing, but for these students to write anything cursively was an accomplishment that required an effort equal to that expended by an intelligent person to attain the highest academic award. It is in this general context that the following discussion of specific accomplishments in writing needs to be assessed.

1   *Improvement in the motor skill of writing*
Once they left school most students rarely practised their writing and consequently their actual script was usually extremely childish. A typical comment from tutors and students was that:

> He (I) can get along perfectly without having to write and spell.

Nevertheless most students learned enough to write out short notes to the milkman or simple *aide-mémoires* to help them in their work, and although they never seemed to cease being nervous when they picked up pen or pencil, the typical progress was registered as follows:

> Originally he was printing and now he is writing in script. He only prints when he becomes worried and agitated and only if he is having a lot of trouble in working out the words. Otherwise, he is writing legibly and his letters are so well formed that there is no doubt as to what is meant by his writing. I am quite happy about that!

or:

> His writing is much quicker and more sort of fluent. Not so angular. It was very laboured and rather large and he still does not put the loops on the 'l's. He says he was told not to do that at school, but I pointed out that it might be an 'l' or a 't' if you have forgotten to cross it. *But I think he will never learn that.*

or, as the student put it:

> As far as putting pen to paper is concerned, it is becoming easier now. It's not quite there!

But many students were able to write perfectly well:

> His handwriting? Quite good. It has always been all right, in fact it is that of an average adult in cursive style.

On occasions the tutor allowed the student to sacrifice his standard of handwriting in the interests of giving him more practice in spelling and sentence construction. An interesting account of such a dilemma which continually, and particularly, faces the tutor of adults is that of an experienced tutor/organiser who said:

> His handwriting has got worse but *what* he is writing has improved fantastically. Once upon a time, he would never write anything at all without looking at it and copying it. I am now giving him spelling tests. Now that is a great achievement because he was so unsure of himself and so afraid that he could not possibly do anything at all. Now I have proved to him that he can. It is remarkable. So writing, yes. I think, to pot with the handwriting at the moment. What is coming out is good. We are moving it.

In fact, as the above quotation shows, most tutors aimed for improvements in spelling and most students hoped to achieve this as their major aim.

2 Improvement in spelling

Some organisers of literacy schemes have suggested that many students admit to being poor spellers but, in fact, they are also poor readers and poor writers. This may have been true of a minority of students, but the evidence of the students seen suggested that most of them were quite truthful in this self-analysis. They could read better than they could write; they could hardly write any extended piece of text if they could not spell and progress in this aspect of writing was greatly appreciated. How much it mattered to students is clearly explained in the next quotation from a student:

> There is no way in which anyone can experience not being able to read or write. I feel that much different . . . it is still the small, silly little mistakes that I am making that I could have learned when I was ever so young. But since I've come here, I have been

learning the words that I would use today. I have less difficulty with the harder words than the silly little small catchwords. But I'm getting to the stage where a couple of times at work, quite out of the blue, someone has asked me, 'How the devil do you spell so and so?' Before, I would have gone off to the toilet quickly without hesitation. But now, I've been fortunate in these couple of instances and known how to spell the word. *It does wonders for your ego!*

But spelling remained their greatest hurdle; in fact, very few students ever seemed to reach the proficiency of being able to write a two-page script. The usual student was more likely to be properly described in one of the four assessments given below. Of student A, the tutor said:

> She still has great difficulty in combining the sounds that make up a word and her spelling and her writing, therefore, are just as slow as ever and there is no progress. She does not have a chance to use it in her social life or occupation.

and student B:

> Well now, his writing is still laborious. He can *copy*. But if he wants to write something of his own invention, then it is a slow process to which he has to give terrific attention, and even then he will look at his tutor for help.

and student C:

> . . . has made pretty well nil progress . . . still only writes in block capitals and she knew that before she came to us. She does not have the competence to imagine a word, how it looks.

and student D:

> She is slightly worse than student C; no progress.

Those students who started off with higher levels of writing skill rarely improved very much further in actual spelling skill; that is, when not using aids. For example:

> I seem to learn the big ones better than the small ones (words). Yes, I can get them down on paper – *my handwriting* has improved a lot.

or:

> I can write a bit more – it's the spelling that comes unstuck, you

> knowl I could write a lot better if I knew how to spell the words better.

or even a student who became an aide to other students:

> I find I can write things down much better now, without having to think about it. *Still a bit slow at doing it; I have to have time;* I find I can do it on my own without having to ask quite so many *spelling* questions, you know. I think, *other than that,* I am doing quite well.

3 Improvement in the ability to check spelling

Consequently many tutors' attitudes changed and more emphasis was placed on how to approach the problem of literacy and on using aids:

> They have got, as an achievement, an *approach* to solve their problems later . . . you give them a framework in which they can think about *spelling* and reading and you help them to realise that most things that are written they can use. . . .

> Well, undeniably, an ability to see the problem as something they have to contend with rather than that they were thick.

Thus, tutors often emphasised how to check spelling and how to use aids to spelling, and the ability to use a dictionary was frequently mentioned as an achievement by both tutors and students. To give but three examples of their opinions:

> His determination is to get on with the bigger words because he is learning *dictionary skills* and we are working a lot on the dictionary.

> I have to have a dictionary handy, just to make sure!

> Obviously there are some words that I cannot do, but I can work round these with the help of a dictionary.

4 Improvement in the ability to take dictation

Improvements in this skill were judged to demonstrate that the student was more capable of dealing with the phonic processes. At the same time, many tutors used dictation as a means of helping the student write a more extended piece of text. Usually the dictation passages were extremely simple. The normal use of dictation was described as follows:

> It is very difficult for them to learn spelling so it always seems easier to teach reading. If I am going to give somebody some

work – a dictation, for example – I find a book that they can read easily, but they will not be able to spell half the words. Thus, I go to an *easier* book to give them practice in taking dictation.

Incidentally, that is what we are doing – this Blackwell Reading thing – the one with a word and a sentence. He likes me to dictate to him so that he can practice his spelling. He wants dictation because he knows that if he writes it, he is just copying. He is working *considerably slower than a lot of people* but he is getting a lot of satisfaction out of it, because it is what he wants to do!

5   *An ability to complete commonly-used forms*
Many tutors made enquiries about which administrative forms were used by their students; these ranged from application forms for a car licence to those for social security grants. Frequently the students were drilled sufficiently to complete such a form and to some students and tutors this was their major achievement. For example, one student said:

Interviewer: How does this class help you?

Student: Well, filling up forms, that is my problem. I have a lot of hospital forms, rebate accounts, and I would not have done it on my own. But now I can do it better but I still have to get the social worker to check on what I do. Apart from that I think I am improving slowly.

Interviewer (later in the conversation): Is this helping you in any other way?

Student: Forms and things like that – I can read my knitting patterns now – it's helping there.

6   *Improvement in the ability to write letters*
Similarly, tutors tried to make their tuition more germane to the lives of their students by helping them to write a letter which they really wished to post. A typical example of this, as an achievement, was reported by a tutor:

But she wrote to her boy friend when he was away. This was the very first letter she had written. She wrote the letter with some help from me in the class, but she was able to write to him and she was quite pleased about that.

However, it is worth noting, at this point, that these enactive achievements in writing took place in the presence of, and with the help of, the tutor. When it came to doing things for themselves and by themselves, it was quite a different matter.

7 Improvement in the ability to write extended texts

A few students (perhaps more than originally suspected) could be described as being reasonably literate before they joined the scheme. One such case was reported by a tutor:

> The first time he wrote, he wrote something that he considered to be a good GCE model, a beginning and an end, linking. It was quite obvious that the lad had been trained to pass examinations based on a marking scheme. There were sufficient interesting phrases and so on, but even when he relaxed his English was still good. *It was always competent and coherent.*

or, more usually:

> To my amazement he produced a four-page foolscap account of a fishing trip. It had a whole lot of spellings wrong but it was most entertaining reading; it was very graphic. It was unorthodox in places but it was vivid, real writing and he staggered himself by doing it. And the week after that he just could not do a thing – he seemed to absolutely tire himself out by that! And we had to go back to the beginning and plod through worksheets. . . . I thought that I would get less able students and that we would have to go to the very beginnings of phonics.

But the average students rarely wrote an extended piece of work or an essay; all they accomplished was:

Tutor: I asked him to write a brief account of some activity on his own. Such as going to the seaside. I got about four lines: 'I went to the seaside. I saw. . . . We went in the car and it rained. We had a picnic on the beach. We looked at the shops. Then we came home. When we got home it was 7.30.' You know, that sort of thing.

Student (interviewed separately): Writing is, well – I don't do a great deal of writing. I fill in my worksheets every week but *I do not do a lot of writing so my main concern is reading.*

Thus, the students normally progressed only a little in their writing skills, whatever their starting point. Their reading skills tended to improve more, but it emerged that even the skill achievements were more a matter of building up confidence than anything else.

3 Confidence through skill tuition

It is undeniable that some progress in the actual technical skills is a proper requirement of a literacy scheme; but it is also true that little or no progress in the technical skills may be far outweighed by gains in confidence from joining classes and meeting people who share the students' technical problem.

Indeed, as time passed, the schemes specifying one-to-one tuition at home recognised this fact; for example, a social evening organised by one such organisation was reported in these terms:

> . . . a tremendous number of pupils came . . . such a successful party . . . I think the social ease was something really worth hanging on to – unbelievable!

It seems that the greatest gain comes from the act of sharing rather than the skill. One tutor/organiser expressed this fact strongly and lucidly in the following conversation:

Interviewer: But when we come to reading, spelling and writing, there is not much change?

Tutor: No, I'm afraid not. That is, after the first, say, three or four months, when they were brought out of complete *inability* or *some ability* to where they would have been if they had gone to school. But other than that each student seems to have come to a point (after 18 months) where they say: 'This is as much as my brain can do! It cannot cope with complications any more.'

Interviewer: So really, what they have done is to meet people outside their normal lives, to widen their knowledge of life, and if we called it 'adult education' and suggested that they should learn the skill of carpentry or sewing, in a class, then you could say the prime achievement would have been the same?

Tutor: Yes, *even if they had not learned carpentry*, that's right. Oh, yes, it would have still been worth while. It has been worth while from the social point of view of *all* those students – widening their vision, widening their experience and their knowledge of how other people live, talk and read. Yes, certainly. Therefore they are *better educated people.*

The bedrock of self-confidence and of self-awareness emerges again, but nevertheless there are confidence factors resulting from the learning of literacy skills. These are exemplified by:

1   an increase in concentration during tuition;
2   a diminution of anxiety with regard to literacy;
3   an expression of enjoyment in reading and writing;
4   an expression of an expectation to succeed in the literacy skills.

1   *An increase in concentration during tuition*

Most students found it difficult to concentrate for any length of time. However, after a period of tuition lasting 18 months or more, it was found that the concentration of some students, though by no means the majority, had improved and that they could work for up to half-an-hour without a break. *Most* tutors found that the major difficulty they faced was to get their students to concentrate, particularly after a holiday or other gap in regular tuition:

> . . . a nine-week break, then we had to go back a long way.

although increases in concentration during tuition were rarely mentioned:

> He can concentrate for longer periods during lessons – there does seem to be an improvement there.

2   *A diminution of anxiety with regard to literacy*

Many students, particularly those working in groups, reported that they felt less anxious about their literacy problem; for example:

> But now I don't seem to mind; everybody is in the same boat.

or:

> I've got over it because I am talking to *you* about it *now*!

or:

> I must try to cure my reading problem and I do not like to talk about it because it upsets me and if anybody says anything about my reading, I fly off the handle. I still do it, *but I do not do it as much as I used to do.*

or:

> I mean, I got a little card in my window and the lady across the road said to my next-door neighbour, 'What does that mean? Does it mean that he will help you to read?' 'No,' she said, 'he goes to night classes and since he has been to night classes he is reading a lot better – he is reading a lot better than he used to.'

or:

> I keep a pen in the car now – I have one within reach which I did not before, for the simple reason I might have to use it.

3 *An expression of enjoyment in reading and writing*

So far as most students were concerned, the skill of reading never came easily, but a few actually reached the stage when they could say they enjoyed reading:

> We are trying to improve his spoken words and to increase his enjoyment of more difficult words. This he is doing. . . .

> He is actually enjoying reading (the books). . . .

But so far as writing was concerned, no student interviewed stated that he *enjoyed* writing. The most favourable views expressed were merely that they could now write 'to fulfil such and such a task'. Nevertheless, many students increased in confidence through learning just enough writing skills to deal with the situations in which they were *required* to write, few though those occasions were.

4 *An expression of an expectation to succeed in literacy skills*

Many students showed great perseverance, especially when receiving group support, and part of their confidence was based on a stubborn belief in eventual success. After four years, one said:

> This made me say that there is such an improvement. I am confident enough to keep coming to this place.

or:

> Oh, yes, it is coming but it still looks like being a long job. Yes, it is! I hope to read properly some time. I do not think there is any time limit on it. You cannot rush it.

or:

> Yes, it is a lot of time, but I don't look at it as time really. I just look at it – well, as long as I get the reading; I am not too worried about the writing as long as I can read. If it takes another 12 months or two years, perhaps, I will go on!

Summary

Nearly all tutors and students, looking back, said that they felt the achievements had been in:

(a) general confidence;

(b) confidence associated with literacy skills;
(c) reading; then
(d) writing

in that order.
The criteria of cognitive achievements identified in this chapter are:

Reading
An increase in:
1 word recognition skills;
2 sentence recognition skills;
3 comprehension skills;
4 the ability to read informational texts;
5 the ability to read texts beyond the purely informational levels;
6 the ability to read newspapers.

Writing
An improvement in:
1 the motor skill of writing;
2 spelling;
3 the ability to check spelling;
4 the ability to take dictation;
5 an ability to complete commonly-used forms or questionnaires;
6 the ability to write letters;
7 the ability to write extended prose texts.

Confidence associated with skills
1 an increase in concentration during tuition;
2 a diminution of anxiety with regard to literacy;
3 an expression of enjoyment in reading and writing;
4 an expression of an expectation to succeed in the literacy skills.

It has been shown that the major skill achievement was, indeed, in reading, and that achievement in writing was of a lower order, possibly because, in the students' subcultures, encoding was not regarded as an essential feature of the environment. However, although students performed tasks with their tutors, one of the real purposes of education is to provide the ability to act independently; the next chapter deals with the degree of achievement in this respect.

VII Enactive achievements

The evidence in this chapter is based upon what both students and tutors *said* the students actually did outside the ambience of the classroom or the tutorial session. From their statements, 10 criteria of enactive achievement emerged, each of which will be discussed below.

1 The use of reading skills

There was a vast range of achievement in the general use of reading, starting from the rather humble:

> He looked into shop windows and occcasionally saw something that he could read, and at the names on buses – it was very basic but it was an achievement!

To the real achievement of the enjoyment of books as expressed by an exuberant student in the following quotation:

> Well, I have not done much writing . . . no, I can pick up the phone . . . my daughter wrote the letter to ——. I read books now . . . the reading is marvellous.

But to obtain a more detailed view of reading achievements, questions were asked about the actual use of:

(i)   libraries
(ii)   newspapers
(iii)   books
(iv)   the extent to which they read to their children, and
(v)   the use of reading at work.

(i) *Use of libraries*

Out of 19 replies to this question, six said that they had joined a library and these six students were enthusiastic; for example:

> We have just joined the library. I can go and pick a library book. I went to the woman and whispered to her that I was 'On the Move' (BBC series for illiterate adults). I read *Jane Eyre* and it was a super thing. I felt as if someone had given me a pound note!

and:

> She had been here two years and she found out from me the library was free. She kept on saying, 'Beautiful library, beautiful library free!' She was really thrilled. They have some Asian books as well.

and:

> She reads herself, goes to the library and actually buys books.

The remaining 13 replies were usually short:

> Been to a library? No!

but two of the 13 students used their children to obtain books to read. For example, the clear:

> My children get the books; *I* don't go!

or the rather ambiguous reply:

> I've come out of (left) the library; but I do go myself. I get a bit mixed up. *My daughter picks books for me.*

The proportion of students *not* using the library service was probably greater than the 68 per cent suggested by this sample. Many students were not asked directly about their use of libraries because it was quite clear during the interview that this question would embarrass them.

(ii) *Reading a newspaper*

Reading a newspaper was often stated as an objective by tutors and many students wished to do so, perhaps not so much because of their interest in the news but rather because to be seen to be doing so would be a public affirmation of their ability to read. Thus a tutor said:

> My student is taking a paper to work.

> He doesn't take an interest in current affairs so I do not think he will read the national newspapers.

and a student asked her tutor:

> 'How long will it be before I can read a newspaper?' She did not realise that it would take a long, long time!

The typical student, however, struggled through bits of newspapers, registering some new-found achievement:

> I read newspapers – a little bit. Before I used to look at the pictures . . . *The Sun*!

and:

> Read a newspaper? Well, I read bits, mostly the ads because they are all the same letters (similar words).

Nevertheless other students had the ability to read newspapers if they wanted to do so, and some actually did:

Interviewer: Could she read *The Guardian*?

Tutor: Yes, she could. I don't know that she would want to but she could. She could write the 500 most common words; spelling was her problem.

and:

> I read *The Sun*.

and:

> Now I can read a newspaper at home.

and:

> I can read a newspaper; I couldn't do that before.

One student considered the newspaper as a rather soft option; he said:

> I read only magazines, not newspapers!

Another student, who must have started at a fairly high level of literacy, bounded ahead:

> By the end he was reading more in *The Guardian* than I was reading. He would ask if I had read various articles in *The Guardian* and I just had not time to read them.

But *The Guardian* reader was really very exceptional; not only was the student who read only parts of newspapers typical:

Interviewer: Read a newspaper?

Student: No, because they are too small for me.

Interviewer: Headlines, then?

Student: Yes, I can read some of it.

but a large proportion of students, even after nearly two years of tuition, never reached the stage of doing so. For example:

> Reading? Better than I expected but he cannot read a newspaper.

or:

> He has not got to the stage of reading newspapers!

or the student who thought that newspapers were comics:

> I can read a bit of the papers, my son's comics.

However, many of those who could read newspapers went forward to reading books.

(iii) *Reading books*
A few students could read fluently before they joined the scheme; one commented:

> I read before I came here. I read historical novels usually – Jean Plaidy books.

However, those students who read a book during the period of attendance probably did so for the first time, and their achievement was usually hesitant and often surprising to their tutors:

I try to read books but it takes me a while to get through them.

and:

I read my first book. . . .

and the register of pleased surprise:

He is reading a book – and is *actually interested* in it!

Many of the students read do-it-yourself manuals, recipe books or books concerned with their work. Features of this type of reading were that it was of practical value to the student and that the student could read a section: students were not sufficiently accomplished to indulge in reading extensively. The books that were named were usually simple stories:

I did read a cowboy book at work and I was quite chuffed at that; it was the first time I had ever read a book.

or presented in fairly easy versions, as is the case of children's books such as the 'Ladybird' series. However, a few students read adult books of an undemanding nature:

I read stories like 'Sea Change' and that.

and:

I believe he said he was reading the James Herriot books.

and:

I read a book by Lillian Beckwith, *The Hills is Lonely*.

and:

She bought *Summer of 42* – but she has a comprehension problem and really likes reading Enid Blyton.

A very few students were encouraged to read, and did read, books requiring an emotional response; one student said, rather proudly:

I started to read poetry!

but, regrettably, few students seemed to be able to *comprehend* the meaning of texts which could be described as even slightly sophisticated.

(iv) *Reading to their family*

Most students, mainly women, who claimed to read books had read a children's book aloud to their own child and this was, to them, a tremendous accomplishment; indeed, only a few students managed it.

> I read aloud to my little girl.

and:

> I read to my children, but *I don't know every word*.

> He is reading (her son, aged seven) and I find *now* that I do not hesitate so much when I am reading to him.

and, more positively:

> I am reading to (my son) with expression – '*poor* old man, he has *really* hit the dirt hard' – put more feeling into it.

> Yes, I read to my kids nearly every night now. They won't go to sleep without a story. Not now!

(v)   *Use of reading at work*
Very few students used their reading skills directly for work:

> Really, reading does not come into my work!

and:

> I don't use it at work, I have never had to read at work.

and:

> . . . in his job he does not use literacy for any reason.

but the few students who could put their new skill to direct use found it invaluable:

> I can check the names on the equipment I use at work.

and:

> It helps me at work and all that. Instead of going up to my mates and asking them what the word is and all that, I can read the labels (storeman).

2   The use of writing skills

However limited the use of reading skills, far more was done in that field than in the use of writing skills, as has become evident already. One tutor expressed her disappointment:

Interviewer: Has he done anything that suggests he is using his skills?

Tutor: No, nothing at all! Oh, yes, reading the newspapers; but he is *not* using his writing.

The typical attitudes of the majority of students emerge from the following quotations:

Interviewer: Have you used it at all?

Student: No, I don't think so! I do not like my own writing!

or, more typically:

> Writing is not my need; I don't have to do it!

and:

> I have not written any letters to anyone, but you see writing does not come into my work.

(i) *Writing letters*

> Written a letter? No, though I have written one in class.

or:

> Well, I started to write one (a letter) to my father; I sort of finished one but nine out of 10 times my wife sort of reads it through and corrects the mistakes.

Nevertheless, some students tried:

> I wrote a letter to see if I could get a pen friend; a year ago I could have never done that. But they did not reply!

and quite a few wrote postcards to their tutors when they were on holiday. Similarly, quite a few wrote practice letters to their tutors; for example:

> Her letters to me seem to have improved.

Only a few students, however, actually wrote letters independently and for a purpose, and these students were particularly pleased with their accomplishment:

> Now I can do the cheques and bills . . . *I do all the letters.* I have to write letters to school and I do that now.

and:

> She feels *now* that she can write letters to friends without having her husband do it for her. She says: 'It is amazing; I just write as if I am talking to them.'

and, though a fairly painful process:

> I think before I write – I can think better. I wrote to my son in Canada – it took me 10 times to get it word perfect.

(ii) *Completing forms*

The great majority of students avoided filling in any form without some help or without passing it to someone else for completion (for example, wife or tutor), so that they only had to sign their name. For example:

Interviewer: Have you filled in any form?

Student: No, I don't like it. I never have done!

and:

> Forms? My wife fills in the forms.

and:

> Forms? I let my husband do that.

and:

> Filled in any forms? I always take it home and get my wife to help me.

The refusal to complete forms was surprisingly ingrained, for it was not simply a matter of not being able – they were often not willing.

> Though he really was good enough to tackle anything, if someone

presented him with a form he would say, 'Oh, well, I'll take it home.'

However, some students were pleased to be able to complete even a section of a form:

I can write my name and address now!

Other students would certainly complete routine and repetitional forms, such as work time-sheets, and this accomplishment was the one most frequently mentioned. There were a few students who did act independently in this respect:

He will fill in forms, petrol garage forms.

and:

Interviewer: Have you filled in a form for yourself?

Student: Yes, for my driving test, I filled that in myself. I passed first time for my motor-bike.

and:

I can fill up forms which I could not do before. I could do something when I started but it is getting easier now.

and finally, in the case of a more able student:

She is filling up forms; she is writing letters to school, yes, she is filling in the report sheets that they have to send back. . . . Oh, she could write and read very well – she could not spell, that's all.

(iii) *Free composition notes*

Few students actually wrote notes involving any degree of free composition.

A note to anybody? No!

and:

Interviewer: Do you write notes to school now?

Student: Oh, no, I leave that to the missus!

but, to at least one student, a note was a milestone in his life:

Interviewer: Have you written anything outside your work in class?

Student: No! Oh, I left my wife the first note she had ever had!

(iv) *Christmas cards*

The writing of Christmas cards was encouraged by tutors as being a practical use of their students' skill; many students of low levels of skill were able and willing to do this, but in nearly every case in the sample, students received help.

> She did write and send off (with help) Christmas cards.

One or two male students claimed to do it for themselves, but usually Christmas card writing was an occupation left to wives.

Interviewer: Have you written any note?

Student: No, but I wrote my first Christmas card.

(v) *Use of writing skills at work*

Just as few students needed to read at work, so few students needed to write other than simple phrases:

> I do not have to use (write) English in my everyday job at all!

and:

> My job does not mean that I do a lot of writing; just once a week when I make my time-sheet out. There you are!

and:

> He can now write notes; before he had to mark a reject with an 'R'.

> When I took over the machine last week I felt very happy. I put things down like 'dropped a blade' and 'waiting for further instructions'.

However, a few students needed to improve their writing if they were to make progress in their work or, indeed, to continue in their present job:

> I use it at work. I have more confidence in writing reports, which I do frequently. My boss said: 'Only five mistakes which I will

correct, they are too silly for words. You are getting on very well.' I said: 'Oh, thanks!'

and:

I go through an exam for a job! I always wanted to do that, even though the pay was less!

(vi) *Other uses of writing*
Some students began to keep diaries which, originally, they showed to their tutor as an exercise; one student mentioned continuing this practice after the completion of her tuition:

I keep a diary; I do about a page a day.

Another student used her writing skills independently for relaxation, but this was an extremely rare case:

Yes, (laughter) yes, I think I can do a crossword puzzle on my own. I still tend to write it at the side first and then ask. I do *The Sun* crossword and the *Daily Mirror* crossword.

Other enactive achievements

1 *Regular attendance for tuition*
Logically, as tutors often said, students could hardly learn without taking the trouble to attend lessons. In the event, most students, particularly those in groups, attended regularly *when they intended to continue*. As soon as they were satisfied that they had gained all they wanted, the regularity of their attendance tended to decrease until they left.

Thus, the act of attending regularly could be counted as an achievement. Indeed, after a long day's work, it was.

He used to come every week, no matter what.

and:

She comes very regularly – our main problem is that we tend to talk rather a lot than do actual lessons and I feel rather guilty about this.

and:

Well, I look forward to coming. I DO! I dislike missing class when I am on overtime.

2 *Homework*

At the outset of the scheme in 1975–76, many tutors set great store by the completion of homework; in the event, very few students did any homework. The typical response was:

> He did no homework.

and:

> He won't do any homework so we are not getting anywhere.

and:

> He never did any homework . . . he admitted he was really doing it (the course) because it was a *good thing*!

That the amount of homework was never very great is illustrated by the following quotations:

> Homework? Not a lot, I have not that much time. I pick a paper up and have a quick look through it and that sort of thing.

and:

> I get a little each week (homework). I do not give her a great deal – she had a full-time job plus looking after her family.

and:

> He brought some homework. *His wife helped him.*

but the following was typical of a few students:

> I do homework. I usually take it up to bed and do it when the children are in bed.

There was the exceptional student, spoken about with some awe, who:

> . . . just enjoys reading at home. We did some word building exercises from 'Common Sounds' and he did more of them at home – he is just a poor speller, *that's all*!

3 *Display of literacy 'tools'*

One of the signs that a student is intending to use his literacy skills is to carry round the tools of his trade! In fact, quite a number of students did *not* do so.

Interviewer: Do you carry a pen around?

Student: No!

On the other hand, many students showed some pride in their very possession, clearly regarding such acts as achievements. For example:

> Carry a pen?
> Not until recently. I keep one in the car now. I have a pen within reach which I did not have before. For the simple reason I might have had to use it.

and:

> He would go off and buy packets of pens and pencil sharpeners; in fact, he gave me a pencil sharpener.

and:

> One day he took some biros out of his pocket and said: 'Ah, well, I suppose I have become the sort of person who carries biros around in his pocket!'

or:

> But I do carry a notebook in my pocket for work . . . it helps me to memorise things.

4 *Finding directions*

Most students were able to read the common instructions for road users, as in the following case:

> Well, if I want to go to any seaside place round here I can get there. I drive and I am fairly decent on memory – I know where it is! I have always been able to read road signs, 'Halt' and things like that.

Nevertheless, for many students the achievement that they recorded as being most useful was to be able to find their way around with greater facility; usually it was a mere matter of street names:

> I can read a notice at work . . . and road signs now, but usually I get my transport manager to read them to me.

> I can pick out street names. I could not do that before.

Interviewer: Can you get to a small village outside, say, Norwood?

Student: Yes, I think I could make it. I can go by the lettering.

Interviewer: Would you have been able to do that when you first came?

Student: No, no! I would not!

A few students reached high levels of achievement and were actually able to plan routes from maps. A tutor clearly was pleased with her student's progress in this respect when she said:

> He has even been planning a holiday which he knows he will not take. Looking at maps and planning his routes and what he would find.

5 *Consumer activity and purchasing methods*

Many students were able to shop quite easily, either because they could read:

> Shopping? Oh, yes, I can manage that all right. I can read!

or because they had their own system:

> Shopping? You don't need to read the labels. I know the shape of the bottle; HP means the Houses of Parliament, you can see the picture. If there is no word you look for the first letter, H!

But equally, a large proportion of students either improved or were able to perform purchasing operations for the first time, though still in a very limited way. For example:

> 'I can go shopping without my wife,' so he said. I think that is quite an achievement for him.

and:

> Well, I can go and find wheat flour. I look at the package and break up the words. My husband stood there and said: 'Yes, that's the one you wanted.'

and:

> Now I can write the loaves of bread I want today or if I don't want any bread – things like that.

and:

> I cannot write a shopping list but I can read it.

The great majority of students used cash to make payments but, with the spread of the cheque system, some students managed to use their cheque books at the point of purchase for the first time. However, the reluctance to use cheques was often put quite strongly:

She has always had a Trustee Savings Bank book so that you did not have to sign cheques. But now they are bringing in a cheque book system – *she does not want to have anything to do like that.*

Signed a cheque? No. I can do my name. I could do it before I came here!

or:

Written cheques? No!

But the importance of cheque writing as an achievement is shown by the following five quotations:

Cheques, I wrote the cheques – I was surprised at myself!

and:

I can go out and write a cheque (in a shop).

and:

I can now write cheques!

and:

Yes, I have a cheque book and sign cheques all right, though I take my time.

and:

I can write my cheques quite easily – no stopping . . . I have to think about the word 'twelve'.

Some students only managed to use the postal order system:

I can send a postal order. I do that myself. I cross them and make payment. I did not do that before.

In a rare case, a student applied his literacy tuition to a complex transaction and was pleased with his successful enterprise:

No, not really. I have not written any letters, apart from the fact that there are bills and so forth. Oh, yes! I just recently wrote a letter to —— asking them to do a transaction for my mortgage. *It worked out quite well* – but I had to use a dictionary.

The quotations illustrate that the actual use of literacy in consumer affairs was of a very simple order. Most of the students continued to shop by brand name or bottle shape, and most continued to use cash or left it to their spouse to sign the cheques.

Of equal importance are the activities *not* mentioned by the students; for example, no student mentioned reading hire-purchase agreements, which seems to confirm the conclusion that the actual use of literacy skills in consumer activities was generally very limited.

6 *The critical appraisal of communications media*

Since the main forms of communications media consist of newspapers, radio and television, students were asked about their use of, and their views on the reliability of, each type of medium.

In fact the vast majority of students did not accomplish the level of reading skill described as 'reading comprehension' and a typical response was:

> I listen to the radio more because when I read it off the papers I get mixed up.

Nevertheless a minority of students were able to compare the various types of media and to make appraisals. One student compared some of the popular newspapers:

Interviewer: Has reading made you question things?

Student: Yes, because I find that I can get the full story from the paper and I find it reasonably corresponds with what I heard on the radio. I like to buy *The Sun*; I used to buy *The Express* because I find, funnily enough, the financial side at the back interesting – not that I get involved in it! '*Mirror*' *sort of fails me*; it is more advertising and more propaganda and that sort of thing than basic news.

Other students preferred newspaper accounts to the television versions of events; for example:

> I do not watch TV that much. The papers put it much more to you; the television leaves out a lot.

and:

Interviewer: Do you think that what the papers say is different to what is said on the television?

Student: Oh, yes; it is different news, entirely different! I mean there are two different opinions. Television used to be my world, I was like a cabbage. Now it's not. Anything I wanted to know was on the telly. News – I listen to the news but now I can read it in the paper.

Yes, I have noticed the TV account is not the same as in the newspaper. It was Curry (the ice-skater) when he said he was going to give it up – on the telly! When you read it in the newspaper, he was thinking of going professional. *The paper gave a fuller story.*

On the other hand, other students preferred television accounts to those in newspapers and were extremely sceptical about the press:

I am always very sceptical about what I read – I read *New Dawn* and *The Express* – politics is like football; it depends on which side you are on! I read (an article) in a Sunday newspaper about a chap who said, 'This is me, this is "Cathy Come Home"' – that was a load of tripe, I knew him! That was – years ago.

and:

I used to get it all from the TV. I would rather see it on the telly because I think you get a true picture – I do not trouble with the papers because they put in a lot of things what people do not say. The tape you are taking now says what I say, whereas the newspaper reporter makes his story and therefore he puts things in to suit his story.

One exceptional student compared a television play with the book she had read; she appreciated the written version as being more sophisticated.

Interviewer: Do you feel the book is true to life?

Student: Much truer to life than the actual TV series were. . . .

Thus, among students there were as many different preferences for various media as one would expect to find in the adult population as a whole, but, so far as these students were concerned, literacy tuition had to some extent enabled them to exercise some critical view of the media.

7 *Action taken to ameliorate physical deficiencies*
The most common physical deficiency revealed was poor eyesight, and

one of the results of coming for literacy tuition was the recognition of the need for spectacles. In a sense, the wearing of spectacles was, to the student, much the same as carrying around a pen. Being without spectacles was an excuse for not reading; thus, the action of wearing spectacles was a public declaration of a willingness to read and, in this sense, an achievement. The difficulty of persuading students to wear spectacles can be gauged from the fact that two of the three following quotations register a lack of success:

He needs glasses but *he won't use them*.

and:

I tried to persuade him to have an eye test, but *whether he did I do not know*.

and:

He has gone to the family doctor and optician for glasses.

8 *Movement from paired tuition at home to group tuition*

The impression was given that students did not, on the whole, use their skills other than within the period of tuition. Taken with the other evidence, this may have been due to a lack of confidence when in public and it seemed that, perhaps, the most important enactive achievement was to move from a solely student/tutor relationship to a group situation.

Quite often the paired system of tuition created conditions inimical to student independence:

What he really needs now is a class or group. But he resists the idea.

She would not join a group, I am pretty certain of that. Not even a group with one-to-one tuition – no, I'm sure she would not. (Why?) . . . embarrassment I suppose, really. She would not even see the organiser for lessons while I am away on holiday. She would not consider it at all. She *really* was very *upset* at the thought of somebody else teaching her.

However, some students did move into groups for tuition or attend group socials for paired students at home; for example:

She has gone with a friend to form a group in the local authority organised scheme.

and:

Tutor: We had a shot in the dark, the tutors and the pupils came to a social – a film was shown followed by literally a party. A tremendous number of pupils (*sic*) did come, with and without their tutors. I have never seen such a successful party!

This statement was confirmed by students who attended:

Interviewer: Did you go to the party for tutors and students?

Student: Yes, great, really interesting!

It would be too optimistic to deduce that the move to group tuition was always successful. Very much depended on the way the group was organised, and on whether the level of the group tuition was appropriate for the student. One student left a group in which each student had a tutor, to join a group taken by one tutor. There were several reasons why the move was inappropriate and these are implied in the student's own account:

I started to go to the GCE class next door. Now the teaching there was very efficient but there was no room for a laugh and a joke if you made a mess of anything. But in here, where we are now (this is why I have come back!), it is a nice, friendly atmosphere. Everybody gets on!

Summary

Ten criteria of enactive achievement were identified as:

1   The use of reading skills as shown by:

(i)   using the library services
(ii)   reading newspapers
(iii) reading books
(iv)   reading to any member of the family
(v)   reading instructions at work.

2   The use of writing skills as exemplified by:

(i)   writing letters
(ii)   completing forms, including cheques and payment slips
(iii) writing free composition notes
(iv)   signing Christmas cards and addressing envelopes
(v)   using writing skills at work.

3 Regular attendance for tuition.
4 Completion of homework assignments.
5 Public display of literacy 'tools' (pens, pencils, etc.).
6 General use of literacy skills in locating places from street signs or maps.
7 Uses of communications relevant to consumer choice and payment systems.
8 Ability to evaluate the reliability of various communications media.
9 Action taken to ameliorate physical deficiencies such as wearing spectacles.
10 Movement from paired tuition at home to some form of group tuition.

When the schemes started the category 'enactive achievements', largely derived from tutors' views of the meaning of functional literacy, was third in the list of aims. After a period of two years, and the experience of the students' limited independent enactive achievement, tutor/organisers revalued their priorities and any specific enactive achievement became less important. As an LEA tutor/organiser said: 'Tutors start by thinking they are going to teach straightforward English. As time goes by they switch to adult education.' And a tutor/organiser in a voluntary scheme said: 'We have got to give them *an approach to solve their problems later*. I talk to other tutors *now* and ask them what they are working towards and they seem to agree!' As one percipient tutor expressed it: 'And certainly, to my knowledge, they were not doing much work. But very much was gained in self-confidence. It would follow from that that they may *have gained in self-confidence and social aspirations* and they may *start* reading (and writing) quite soon. Because of this! Because they are a lot more confident.'

In the next chapter the socio-economic achievements, linked to the social aspirations mentioned above, will be considered.

VIII Socio-economic achievements

1 Getting a better job in terms of more pay

At the start of this literacy research in 1975, many tutors thought that, through increased literacy skills, their students would enhance their employment opportunities. For example:

> Most of them come with the hope that when they have done this, they will be promoted. . . .

However, at the end of two years most tutors realised that the increment in skills was generally not of the order to lead to 'better' employment and that, in any case, employment opportunities for individuals often depended on national and international levels of economic activity.

Students, on the other hand, seemed to have been consistently more realistic; the typical student is described in Jaques' song in *As You Like It*:

> Who doth ambition shun
> And loves to live i' th' sun,
> Seeking the food he eats
> And pleased with what he gets.

or, more prosaically, as a tutor said:

> As far as he was concerned there was no such thing as promotion. He was very happy in his job and he had no intention of giving it up!

Another tutor thought that his student was earning quite a substantial income anyway:

He gets about £100 per week (1975 values) though I am not sure if that is his actual take-home pay.

In fact, in contrast with the students who said that:

But wherever you go, you find that the reading (lack of) pulls you back whatever you do (at work).

and:

When you are offered promotion in a job and you know you can do it but you can't write, so you turn down the job. No one can tell you it does not matter! You have just talked your way out of a good job!

six students stated, quite categorically, that their 'problem' had made no difference to their employment. For example:

The reading problem has not stopped you getting work?

No, not at all. I like the job I have got; I just better myself each time I get a new job.

and:

I was never refused a job because of my writing (lack of).

and:

No, it has not stopped me getting a job.

or:

Has it stopped you doing something you would like to do?

No, I like to be outside (in my work).

or:

He tried to hold me down because I could not do the paper work and said I was not worth the money. So I moved out and got a better job.

Not stopped me from getting another job for the simple reason I have never tried.

As usual, there was the marked exception to the general rule:

> She had to give up a job ... she was offered an area managership at £5,000 a year (1975 values).

Nevertheless quite a number of male students wanted to reburnish and improve their literacy skills in order to *retain* their present job; for example:

> They have been laying off blokes; if I am made redundant I can't go back down 10 years. This is what I am afraid of; but they keep saying 'Don't worry'. I don't want to go down the ladder again. I am in charge of seven blokes.

and:

> He wanted the skills for his job.

and:

> He wants it for his business.

Similarly, a number of women felt that they required a better standard of literacy to *retain* their jobs; for example:

> Also it is a business thing – she says in the business world, you have to be careful and if you cannot read you can so easily be done.

and:

> She got what she wanted to run her business.

and:

> She needs to take telephone messages down for her husband's business.

However, a few students had aspirations:

> I would like to get a better job.

and:

> I want to set up my own business.

and:

> I want to be a manager.

and:

> She wants a better job . . . she is very aware that the job she has got is below her . . . she would like to work in a shop.

and:

> He would like to be the manager of the catering section but he cannot because he cannot write very much down.

and:

> I would like to go into office work.

But in the sample only two students stated that their increased literacy had directly helped them obtain higher pay. One had apparently been taken on as a 'disadvantaged' employee at a fairly low wage rate; on proving that he could be more effective, because he could now read package labels, he said that he persuaded his employer to give him a 20 per cent increase. And the other stated:

> Now I have a better job because if I had not learned a bit of reading – got on better with my reading – then I would not be able to do the job I do. You see, I got on because of my reading classes. . . .

The majority of students, however, had jobs that did not require more than the basic reading skills, which they already possessed. Therefore, getting more pay as a *direct* result of literacy tuition was extremely rare.

2   The capability of re-entering the employment market

Many women took a long-term view. Though they rarely went into employment on 'finishing' their course, they prepared for a return to work when their children would be attending full-time school; for example, a tutor/organiser noted that:

> And they (the women students) also do it so that they can get a job when the child's gone to school.

and students:

When the children are all at full-time school I could perhaps go on to A level and go in for typing; not just copy-typing but secretarial:

and:

We had a couple of deaths in the family then and it made you realise . . . panic a bit . . . you thought: 'Heaven forbid that anything should happen' (to her husband) – but . . . *it's an insurance* – I thought, 'It's up to me!'

But of the women students a fairly large proportion had to face the implications of a broken home and these students desperately needed every skill they could muster to support themselves and, in many cases, their families. Most tutors stated their student's predicament fairly starkly:

The reason she joined was to do with home – she has got to face supporting herself.

3 Assumption of greater responsibility at work

Some students learned to write, or to read, enough key words or phrases to enable them to perform basic and usually repetitive tasks, such as entering petrol sales on customers' monthly account cards or completing basic time-sheets for themselves and their 'mates', and these students felt that they had now been allowed to exercise considerable individual responsibility at work. But, for the majority of students, the assumption of greater responsibility at work meant no more than that they did not have to be helped as much as previously; for example:

Oh, yes, definitely. You don't seem so *pushed around* and to have to rely on everybody else. That is what it amounts to.

So you have greater responsibility at work?

Yes, that's right, yes.

Nevertheless, no matter what the circumstances, any small step forward in individual responsibility meant much to the student, and these were examples of considerable achievement.

4 Getting a better job in terms of personal satisfaction and interest

As with many adults throughout the community, some students felt that they would like a more satisfying job, regardless of pay. Two students actually managed to achieve this aim:

> These classes have given me that much courage to get a new job.

Why are you moving then?

> No, I shall be taking a reduction.

More cash in your new job?

> Not so much security . . . it's . . . just a feeling that I will have a job that I think I can enjoy doing and that I can do quite well.

Comradeship?

> Yes, plus the fact that it is a service. It's not a nine to five run-of-the-mill. It's a challenge for life – every minute something different could happen.

and:

> I am passing exams, lower exams but catching up (at work) . . . I have been given the opportunity to go abroad.

Another student had been given help too late in her working life; her story is not just one of individual frustration but is also of high social cost. In her own words:

> I don't want to be a cleaner all the time . . . the happiest time of my life was when I was looking after people, even though it was bedpans and washing for them. . . . I said to the Matron: 'Can I go upstairs as a ward orderly?' And that was marvellous . . . I took those old people to heart – they were mine – it was super. 'Would you like to go to night school (for nursing qualifications)?' said the Matron. She was sweet. But I could not pluck up the courage to tell her that I could not write, so I could not go!
>
>   Then I worked in a children's home. It was a marvellous job but they wanted another housemother. And it meant a lot of writing. Now I could not tell them. In fact I had a nervous break-down. If only I could have said, 'I'm sorry, I want the job but I

can't face all the reports.' I just went berserk. One Friday morning they asked me to sign a paper. I just screamed and that was it!

But for most students a better job in terms of satisfaction was neither required nor attainable. Nevertheless the students had their dreams; for example, one said, rather vaguely:

I hope to change my job – get on and improve.

and yet another, because of his literacy tuition, began to think of converting his dream into reality – perhaps a first step to an actual achievement:

I was somewhat taken aback when he was talking the other day, somewhat tentatively, of setting up a business of his own. I am sure that would not have entered his head when he first came to me.

5   Better relationships in the place of work

In fact the majority of students felt that their conditions of work had improved because their newly-found *confidence* had resulted in better relationships. There was no doubt of the sincerity of their accounts, their appreciation of their tutors' role in this achievement and their somewhat wondrous delight that this should have been a result of their 'literacy work'. Speaking generally about this aspect of their achievements, the following statements were typical:

At work . . . it does wonders for your ego.

So it (literacy) has been used at work?

Oh, yes.

It makes me feel better at work . . . I felt that I was under them and they was above me!

Changed a lot – at work – that helps me at work and all that.

Yes, well I can *talk to* more people *at work.*

It makes a lot of difference at work . . . you don't have to say you have forgotten your glasses any more!

Some students felt that it helped their relationships because they were now willing to turn their hand to other tasks at work or could do their work better; for example:

> I got a great deal out of it. I do honestly. I feel myself . . . well, before it used to hold me back. I used to think twice before I would do a job (at work) . . . I have more confidence in myself.

and:

> I find it easier at work . . . I actually took over the machine last week . . . I can get by on my own now!

and:

> I have got more confidence in writing reports (at my work).

The employers were generally supportive and helpful. One student recorded, with appreciation, that her 'boss' had encouraged her to start:

> The boss said: 'You just go to learn to spell and you would get enjoyment out of it.'

But sometimes the employer's enthusiasm was misplaced, and quite a few students who came because of their employer lacked the personal interest to take advantage of their opportunities and, if anything, were probably worse off as a result. Such students merely repeated their failure at school. One such student was described by a tutor, somewhat acrimoniously:

> The firm had pressurised him to attend to improve his spelling; he was under pressure. He might as well have been out. (The student, in fact, left.)

Furthermore, although many employers were supportive, their foremen, often the students' immediate 'boss', were sometimes less than helpful:

> He is working with a man who knows that he cannot read and keeps rubbing it in: which has made him more tense. . . .

It is interesting to note therefore that in general, when employers initiated the process, students gained very little.

6 Participation in civic duties

Some students began to involve themselves in various civic duties; one student, encouraged by his tutor, accepted his call for jury service.

(a) *Jury service*
He was called for jury service and he talked quite sensibly about it.

On the other hand, another student, whose tutor was less adventurous. was excused. In the words of the tutor:

> We had a long discussion about what he was going to do about this jury service. In the end *I* wrote them a letter . . . (so he did not do it).

(b) *Parent/teacher liaison*
Other students found that their role in the valuable process of parent-teacher liaison had improved. A typical case of this feature of achievement was noted by a tutor who was also a teacher at the school attended by the student's child:

> She is much more able to visit her junior school as a parent.

(c) *Youth club leadership*
Some students began to make a contribution in youth clubs. One student, in fact, thought that the confidence he acquired was best shown by his activity in this field and his main achievement was given as:

> I go along to help with the lad's (his son's) club now.

(d) *Committee work*
However, where the skills, *per se*, were required, students avoided their civic duties; as one student said:

> They asked me to go on a committee but I could *not* do it.

(e) *Voluntary service participation*
This was best illustrated by the case of a lady who could read but still disliked writing, and who joined in activities where writing was rarely required. After two years' tuition, she had gained in confidence to the extent that her tutor could report:

> She has joined the home nursing group ... she has got involved in the local community school – she is very busy. It really is – a success story.

There was one student (a rare case of broken schooling) whose confidence and ability in the skills improved sufficiently for her to become a literacy tutor in a one-to-one group supervised by a tutor/organiser.

Summary

The criteria of achievement that emerged from a consideration of socio-economic activities were:

1 getting a better job in terms of more pay;
2 increasing the capability of re-entering the employment market;
3 the assumption of greater responsibility at work;
4 getting a better job in terms of personal satisfaction and interest;
5 developing better relationships at the place of work;
6 participation in civic duties such as:

(a) accepting jury service
(b) improving parent-teacher liaison at children's school
(c) accepting youth club leadership
(d) accepting committee membership duties
(e) participating in voluntary services.

The great majority of students experienced better relationships at the place of work and many of these assumed greater responsibility at work, usually resulting from their increased confidence to carry out the simpler routine writing or reading tasks.

Quite a few students began to participate, or extended the depth of their participation, in civic duties, particularly those duties concerned with parent-teacher liaison.

A very few students obtained better jobs in terms of personal satisfaction although it was extremely rare to find a student who, because of literacy tuition, had obtained a better job in terms of more pay.

The capability of a few students to re-enter the employment market was only slightly improved by the system of one or two lessons a week in literacy skills. Yet, for some students, there was a desperate urgency in their need to equip themselves to earn an independent livelihood, and it was unfortunate that such students were not re-directed into something like a training opportunities scheme or college of further education where there would have been a reasonable period of tuition every day. Thus, this criterion of achievement, which was obviously so crucial for the students concerned, was not allocated the importance it deserved because the very system of organisation of the literacy campaign militated against success.

Indeed, the success in socio-economic achievements was largely due to the fact that few students demanded *economic* success and that the majority required *social* success. This theme is continued in the next chapter, which deals with affective social achievements, that is, improvements in the students' ability to harmonise the maturation of personal psychology within various aspects of social relationships.

IX Affective social achievements

1 Improved relationships within the family

The most important of the affective social achievements centred on the students' relationships with their families. There are two reasons for emphasising this point.

First, whatever the source of information about a literacy scheme, whether it was from broadcasting, the newspaper or from friends, the student's final decision to enrol was, in the majority of cases, due to the encouragement of one or more members of his immediate family. Five typical examples illustrate this point:

> I think she really persuaded him to do something about It.

and:

> She (wife) got me here.

and:

> His wife used to drag him along.

and:

> He persuaded his sister to come to the class.

and:

> His brother had been encouraging him for some time.

Another student suggested that his desire was to help his son to read, but clearly he only enrolled because of his wife. He said:

> My little lad, yes. *My wife kept on about it* and I kept thinking of it more and morel . . . She is pleased because I come here.

Secondly, students and tutors all recognised the importance of student family relationships and the ameliorative effect that the students' efforts were usually having in these relationships. The evidence of two typical students was very decisive in this respect:

> Easier with your family?
>
> Definitely!

and:

> Is it helping you in your family?
>
> Oh, yes!

as were the comments of three tutors:

> She does feel that she is the one in the family that *can't* (read) because her two brothers and sister can.

and:

> I think better relationships with the family; I would think so from the way he talks.

and:

> We decided that he could now, quite cheerfully, tell his family that he was having lessons with me. It is a curious world, to me, of human relationships!

But these relationships were shifting, changing and complex; though most students claimed an improvement, disappointments and worsening conditions also emerged, sometimes as a direct result of the student's involvement in remedial literacy tuition. One male student's relationship with his son had the quality of a shooting star. His tutor said:

> And then they took the son into their confidence . . . the son just thought that his father was lazy . . . the son started making him do his homework and he started making leaps forward. Then the son got bored . . . and now his son tells his dad that he (the dad) is stupid!

The evidence of these relationships can be categorised into three main groups:

(i)   the student-husband's relationship with his wife;
(ii)   the student-wife's relationship with her husband;
(iii) the students' relationships with their parents.

(i) *The student-husband's relationship with his wife*
Usually the wife's attitude was one of pleasure that her husband had enrolled, and most student-husbands recognised this as an improvement in relationships. For example:

> She (wife) is pleased.

and:

> Before I used to have to ask the wife what it was. She notices the difference now . . . my missus realises it. I know she knows it.

and:

> What does your girl friend think of all this?
>
> . . . I even hid it from her. But she knows now and I get the support I should do.

and:

> His wife's attitude is of general encouragement. I would not think she has put any pressure on him but she is all for him trying to get better.

Many husbands received help from their wives. One tutor said:

> His wife seemed to be helping him.

and a student noted that:

> She prepared a lot of words for me to go through.

Equally often the wife had neither the temperament nor the ability to help her husband, and it seemed that husband-wife relations improved when a tutor entered the scene.

> She is a secretary; she wants to help him but she has not the technical knowledge (to teach literacy skills).

or:

> She tried to help him but she used to lose patience with him,

which was understandable. But when he came to me, his wife was more patient with him.

On occasions, students wished to be independent of their wives' help. The following student looked forward to this when he said:

I wanted to be more independent – my wife has been writing for me so far. . . .

Some students, by enrolling, did not improve their relations with their wives. They may not have become worse, but they had the problem of meeting their wives' expectations:

He wants to live up to his wife's expectations.

Sometimes they had to live in circumstances where a wife feared her husband's disability becoming known. One such couple, neighbourly and socially aware, were placed in such a dilemma when the student enrolled in a scheme; both were worried about being 'found out' and the wife obviously felt very strongly about it. Indeed, the husband's evidence was so vehemently given that, perhaps, it would have been better to have left well alone:

She dreads it; very, very, very worried, as much as I am . . . (at his illiteracy being known in the neighbourhood).

The picture of the supportive wife, benignly giving her husband encouragement, was far from being universally true. It could be argued that if marriage is seen as a joint and equal partnership, then both partners should have been interviewed in the initial stages, and any advice should have been based on broader principles than just the advisability of the student becoming literate.

(ii) *The student-wife's relationship with her husband*
The arguments in section (i) could also apply in some of the following cases. One tutor described a classic case of the well-intentioned husband:

Is her husband supportive?

Yes, he is. At times in the past he has been over-pushing. He has suggested that she go along to night school and on one occasion he enrolled her for a course. He knew the teacher. He enrolled her in a course of typing, which was a very strange thing to do because she went along and went to pieces in the lesson, of course. I think he thought it would help her writing if she could type, but, of course, she does not need that! She reads excellently – no problem in reading. You see, she was 'working class' and is now, I suppose, 'middle class' . . . I am keeping in touch with her but she feels she cannot cope with any work at the moment because of her domestic problems.

Many of the women students sought release from an over-dependence on their husbands' skills and, on the whole, the women's evidence was presented forcibly. For example:

I would say, 'Oh, I wrote a letter to your mother,' and he would sort of go over it and correct it. It used to make me cry and I thought I should have got it right in the first place.

and:

She feels now that she can write letters to friends without having her husband do it for her! Her husband was doing quite well (economically and socially) and she was very nervous.

But most students felt that their husbands provided tolerant encouragement; for example:

He is very helpful . . . when I arrive he clears out of the way and that sort of thing.

and:

He (the husband) was very happy; oh, yes! He says: 'Well, you do it then. It is practice for you.'

and:

She (mother) thinks I have improved a bit and my boy friend, when he hears me read, he says: 'You are getting on better than you used to, because you don't hestitate so much now.'

However, the general impression was that few husbands actually *pushed* their wives into having tuition; many encouraged, but few actually exercised the pressures that wives exerted on their husbands. The most usual attitude was:

Husband approves?

Yes, yes; provided I am happy doing it. He says: 'If it starts to worry you, pack it up!'

(iii)   *The students' relationships with their parents*

Many of the unmarried students said that their parents, especially their mothers, were pleased that they had enrolled. Mothers had usually the task of dealing with their children's schools and, after the frustration of those experiences, many of them felt relieved that their children were taking advantage of a second chance. Consequently relationships between student and mother usually improved; for example:

> Apparently his mother asked all through his school life if he could have special teaching and was told 'No!'

and:

> His mother just seemed to think that he ought to read better – a sort of moral idea! The effort he put into reading was incredible; he used to go red in the face with trying, but it was really his mother who brought him.

or, more usually:

> Does it comfort your mother?
>
> Yes, because she knows that I am not an idiot. She knows that I can get on all right on my own. She was a bit bothered before!

and:

> Family's views?
>
> My mum wants me to come. She feels I am improving and I feel I am improving.

Fathers tended to follow the mothers' lead; for example:

> We are better now, we (student and his sister) never used to get on. Mum and dad are pleased.

There was one case where the father, in particular, was irritated by his son's inadequacies; here the relationship certainly improved:

> I get on with my dad better than I used to do!

2   Reading to their children

A surprising number of students said that their main purpose in enrolling was to learn to read to their own children. On closer investigation, this statement had two distinct meanings:

(i)   to improve their relationship with their children through the act of reading to them, and

(ii) to improve their relationship with their wife by sharing or being able to share, if required, the duty of reading to their children.

(i) *Reading to their own children for its own sake*
Even this fairly simple criterion of achievement contained several layers of perception. Most students simply enjoyed reading to their children:

> Yes, I read to the kids.

> I like reading to the girl.

> My little girl now likes me reading books to her. She is three-and-a-half years old and she sits down and listens to me now.

Other students felt that reading at home was a necessary adjunct to their children's school work:

> It started because her daughter was having problems with phonics. . . .

Yet other students found that reading to their children was a shared experience, in that their children also read to them:

> They read to me actually – of course, I can read the one (book) that he is doing and I am better at it.

And many students, probably the majority, found that their improved relations with their children were part of their more general confidence in their ability to deal with life. Such a feeling of more general confidence is implied in the following two quotations:

> Also I find that I am much more confident now with —— (her son).

> Oh, yes, a lot easier to get on with the kids.

(ii) *Reading to their children as part of their relationship with their spouse*
In general, most students felt that:

> I thought I ought to help the children with one thing or another.

But mothers expressed a feeling of maternal inadequacy because of their lack of literacy and over-dependence on the father, in statements such as:

> (My daughter) says, 'You help me, Mummy,' even when my husband is helping her.

which their tutors corroborated in the following terms:

> Have any of the women said that it is better at home because they can help their children?
>
> Oh, yes. *Certainly.*

and:

> She is much more able to help her children. She does not need to say, 'Well, go and ask your father!' It is good in that respect because she is very attached to her children and she wants to do everything she can. And that was really her motive for starting, anyway.

Similarly, the fathers resented too explicit a dependence on the mother and their statements nearly match those of the mothers; for example:

> Easier at home?
>
> Well it is really, for the children. I read 'Ladybird' books to my son. Before I used to say to them, 'Go and give it to your Mum!'

Such a statement was confirmed once more by tutors, who remarked:

> His children were at the age when they were bringing home home-work. His son was having spelling problems at school and it was always felt that his mother would help him. He was fed up not being able to do his bit.

and:

> I think his pride is hurt that the child goes to the mother and not him.

3 Sharing ideas with others through literacy

A few students were able to use their literacy skills to share ideas with others, as distinct from reading the ideas of the authors. One student used the BBC TV programme 'On the Move' as a vehicle to share ideas with her son:

We used to watch 'On the Move' (BBC TV programme) because it helped the children so well; we *shared* it.

But, more frequently, students learned to share their problem of illiteracy, and in so doing enlarged their own personality. One such experience, typical of the accounts of many students, is that of a student who met a friend who showed embarrassment at being asked to write down a list for a bazaar. In the student's own words:

'Yes,' she said. 'Because I cannot spell.' So I said, 'That makes two of us, Jill.' . . . I was not bothered because I can tell them.

Both humility and confidence emerge from this evidence with, above all, a precious moment of human contact and understanding. To have been able to respond thus was, surely, an achievement.

4 Willingness to put forward own point of view

One of the achievements noted by both students and tutors was the students' increased ability to put forward their own ideas, rationally and in public. Many students remarked on their own nervousness, shyness and reticence, and commented that their relationship with tutors and other students had helped them to converse more readily.

Both my husband and my mother have noticed that I am not so shy. I am better if I have to go out and meet strangers, I can talk more!

and:

I can talk to people better as well.

Other students brought their own ideas to the notice of their group and to their tutor/organiser:

He is trying to hatch ideas now on how we can make some money and make ourselves independent (the centre faced the problem of increases in fees). He had a suggestion for a jumble sale and a suggestion for a bring and buy sale. I have left him to work at some others.

One student who thought, quite correctly, that the solution to a problem posed for group consideration was to enlist some help, stood up and said so, much to her own surprise and delight:

I had the nerve to stand up and say: 'Could I have four strong men?'

whilst another student recorded her progress in this respect as:

I help to run a group (children's playgroup) and I find I am asked to go to a meeting. Instead of just sitting there agreeing with everybody, if I think something is wrong now, I will put my point of view.

Many other students perceived this as an achievement: they argued that their discussion with the research interviewer was, in itself, clear proof of a willingness to put forward their own point of view. This was confirmed by the number of students, usually those in the sheltered one-to-one home tuition nexus, who declined to be interviewed.

5 Improvement in social relationships with fellow students

Since the development of the students' relationships within the group was observed by both tutors and interviewer, the evidence of improvement in this respect may be regarded as probable confirmation of the students' own perceptions of their developing relationships at home and elsewhere.

There was no doubt that the students' ability to handle social relationships improved in the groups attending the adult centres. Although group occasions were infrequent in the voluntary schemes, when students did meet together the tutors noticed the success of those gatherings. However, it was only at adult centres where group behaviour could be *continuously observed* and estimates of improvement attempted; consequently the following evidence refers to students in such groups. Of 10 typical cases, tutors said:

He is much more alive now than when I first came.

or:

He has become far less uncouth.

or:

He is much more outgoing.

and:

He certainly does *now* join in with the group (at the centre).

and:

We have given them sociability – definitely. We have brought them out of a lonely backwoods existence where they had no social contacts.

and:

I think he is coping with life better than he was – he panics – but he does not lose his temper in the same way – he is very edgy, childish in some ways. He is really here for group therapy!

and, as a summary:

His main achievement is a total change in human relationships – I think he handled it (his affair with another student) very well – he has matured.

Summary

The criteria of achievement which resulted from the evidence about affective social achievements were:

1 better relationships with all members of the family;
2 better relationships through reading to children;
3 better relationships through sharing ideas about literacy;
4 better relationships through being willing to put forward one's own point of view;
5 better relationships within tuition groups.

Although tutors recognised the importance of these relationships as the schemes matured, students seemed to know intuitively that this was their principal gain.

I get on with people much better – it is gradually getting better. Well, I don't have so many arguments with people like I used to do.

And a sad but moving tribute to the adult centre:

I have two years' probation – they put me on tranquillizers – *these classes helped me keep going.*

Thus the role of tutors was far from being that of a skilled purveyor of technical knowledge: whether they liked it or not, whether they were qualified or not, they found themselves in the roles of counsellor, friend and listener.

Sometimes the very fact of joining an empathetic group caused the student to question other aspects of his way of life; for example, one experienced tutor/organiser remarked:

> I don't think he is terribly happy in his digs; but there again, that might be something *we have done to him* – I don't know!

But, as has been stated in previous chapters, students seemed to represent the variety to be found in the adult population as a whole, and, so far as social relationships were concerned, the average student was not very different from the average fully literate adult.

Nevertheless many students faced problems, the solutions of which were far beyond the training or experience of the voluntary literacy tutor. A number of students clearly needed the comfort of talking to someone, and saw the literacy symbol as a means of achieving this. For example, some students faced, or had just experienced, a breakdown in their marriage:

> The trouble with my student was that his marriage broke up. He was becoming interested in his children's work – so really, why he wanted to learn was for his children and his wife, and then this was all gone. So the interest had gone, though he got along quite well.

or:

> He was afraid of being an embarrassment to his children, who were teenagers. He has just got diverced.

or:

> He is having domestic trouble; he slept out in the car, left home and then returned home.

An extreme example of such a case was given by one tutor:

> I could not accept the way he was treating his girl friends and thought that someone ought to put it very strongly to him – the idea – someone whom he respected, which I thought he did me – that this girl with whom he was going out was quite obviously in

love with him. I turned myself into a counsellor . . . he decided to sign himself off and said that he had made a lot of progress in English. I said: 'Well I think it depends on what your standards of progress were. After all,' I said to him, looking him straight in the eye, 'you were not just coming for English were you?' He coloured and did not look back at me. So maybe I was too direct in the end, but I did feel that he was the sort of person who would go on sheltering behind me and other friends. I don't know what I should have done. I think I did get very involved with him. I wanted him to go to the counselling sessions that they had in town. . . . I see him in town and he does not recognise me . . . I think he was confused himself; he was disturbed.

Thus the problems were more complex than any remedial literacy tutor could reasonably be expected to handle, and many failures to achieve a modicum of affective social balance were the fault of neither tutor nor student, but rather the result of erroneous expectations on the part of some of the innovators of literacy schemes who under-estimated the need of a counselling service to sift students in their initial contacts. An indication of general problems was given by Marilyn Morgan (1977) when she wrote:

> The third group of students (about 25 per cent) comprises students who were ascertained ESN at school, those with specific learning difficulties or those with a physical handicap (partially-sighted, partially-hearing, etc.).

This proportion was probably also correct for the sample discussed in this investigation, and must always be remembered in any consideration of the problem of literacy.

However, as Bacon wrote: 'They are poor discoverers that think there is no land when they see nothing but sea.' The majority of students were normal people who, in groups, sharing experience with tutors and fellow students, found a new confidence which enriched their social relationships, and on this assumption the emergent criteria will be evaluated in the concluding chapter.

X Emergent criteria of achievement

The objectives of our study were, first, to identify the aims of students and tutors involved in adult remedial literacy schemes; secondly, to discuss the achievements of both illiterate adults and their tutors in relation to their stated aims; and, thirdly, to establish a schedule of appropriate aims (the word 'appropriate' in this context meaning in terms of the philosophy of adult education). This chapter reviews and summarises the attainment of these objectives within the framework of an ethological approach to the subject matter.

(a) Methodological considerations

It has been shown that student members of the literacy scheme represented a variety of levels of competence in literacy skills and consequently the definition of an illiterate adult is an adult who thinks he has a reading or writing problem. The terms of this definition imply that the students wish, first, to improve their technical literacy skills and, secondly, to ameliorate their self-image of inadequacy. The paradox is that although this dichotomy of aims may be stated analytically, in the process of achievement the improvement in skills was often found to be subservient to and dependent upon the enhancement of self-image. Consequently the development of individual literacy skills, like other skills, can take place satisfactorily only within the context of a process of adult education.

This process, usually, is one in which there is an interaction between three constituents: the student, the other students and the tutor. The student brings to the group his own assumptions and conceptions of himself as a unique person. Through his relationships with other students he sees himself mirrored and reflected and, in that respect, as in normal daily 'social' interaction, his reactions will be largely adventitious. However, the student usually expresses a desire to develop in some specific respect, in a skill such as literacy or in an individual emotional or spiritual context as, for example, when a student joins a marriage counselling group.

In this process, from the student's point of view, the tutor has a double role. As a fellow adult, the tutor partly represents another student, who may be a source of competition or be supportive. Nonetheless, the tutor possesses privileges beyond those afforded to the other students and these are based on the student's acknowledgement of the tutor's expertise and on the willingness of the student to allow the tutor to intrude into certain aspects of the student's private psyche. Because the tutor has been granted these prerogatives, the tutor himself, or through his influence on the student group, may moderate the largely accidental influences of the students upon each other, in order to facilitate each individual student's development towards maturity. Thus, whatever the skills being taught, the student's self-image and view of his inadequacy are likely to change, and the adult illiterate may conceivably gain little in a skill achievement but, through the modulation of self-image, learn to deal with his disadvantage.

However, the argument has been advanced that adult education need not take place under the guidance of tutors. A student may learn from daily social contacts or through television and radio or from books. Learning through daily contacts is, as described above, adventitious, and learning through television, radio or books is limited to a one-way form of communication in which the student may neither redirect nor contribute to the process of learning. A student with a literacy problem is handicapped to a greater or lesser extent in profiting from these wider opportunities and, on the evidence, needs direct tuition and sympathetic guidance to reduce the handicap.

Though it is undeniable that all forms of communications media may contribute to adult education, we argue that the written word as a medium is, next to the spoken word, currently the most economical and universal method of conveying instructions or ideas. Particularly because of the use of the written word as a means of transmitting knowledge in its widest sense, it is a contradiction in terms to describe an illiterate person as educated, and in so far as education is a *desideratum*, literacy cannot be regarded as anything other than a basic, essential, universally desirable skill. Furthermore, it is a skill *related* to other manifestations of social activity.

Accordingly there have been sundry international and national initiatives to achieve universal literacy. One of the most recent of these initiatives has been the Adult Literacy Campaign, inaugurated in 1975 in the United Kingdom. The present study has been of the aims of this campaign, the stated criteria of success and the actual achievements of students and tutors in a typical area in the United Kingdom. London and other large cities have special, atypical problems, principally those stemming from inner-city social deprivation and population migrations. Information from other concurrent research projects, primarily from the research conducted by the National Institute of Adult Education, confirmed, however, that the forms and historical development of the services provided in the LEA areas studied and the experiences of tutors and students there were in the most important respects similar to those elsewhere, particularly in England and Wales.

Several methodological approaches were considered, but were rejected as leading to over-simplifications of the nature of the students' perceptions of their problem of illiteracy. Given a spectrum of individual students' abilities, from inability to structure a sentence to sensing inadequacy because of relatively minor spelling mistakes, it became necessary to construct a field of discourse whose boundary encompassed a sense of individual inadequacy. Inadequacy in what? The student expressed it in terms of literacy, but the exciting possibility was that an approach existed which would take account not only of feelings of inadequacy in literacy skills, but of all cases where lack of a skill is the stated reason for such a feeling. Hence the choice of an appropriate methodology for literacy could also be utilised to illuminate perceptual patterns of other disadvantaged groups seeking adult education.

Ethology has, as the boundary of the universe of discourse, the notion of a struggle for genetic survival through behavioural adaptation to the natural and social environment of a species. This notion provides the disciplinary framework within which the processes of the observation of animate behaviour, of the derivation of hypotheses, of the procedures of re-observation and of interpretation are fused. By adopting the ethologists' approach and by redefining survival as meaning that level of self-image which enables a man to cope to his satisfaction with the majority of his practical, emotional and spiritual problems, it becomes clear why there is never any given level of skill which will satisfy all individuals at any particular time. The man with an O level standard of English language who joins a literacy class will be acting rationally if, in his view, such a standard is not adequate for his survival self-image. Similarly, a ukase may not be issued declaring that all who are able to read, for example, page 29 of *War and Peace* will be deemed literate; there will be some for whom that 'objective' standard of literacy is insufficient for survival, as defined in this context.

To adopt the ethological approach is not to allege that man's senses and sensitivities are the same as those of other animals; man is capable of an image of 'God'. Cf. Thorpe (1974). Whatever that image is, it must to some degree affect his self-image, for the very ability to comprehend an idea of 'God' displays an ability to perceive past and future, deception and truth; all constituent factors in any individual's self-image. Thus the ethological approach utilised in this text is a sophisticated derivative of that usually accepted by the naturalist.

Consequently the student who came forward could be considered as having reached a decision to rectify a perceived disadvantage, primarily to alter the perception of disadvantage rather than the identified limitation in skill, and his aims could be interpreted within the framework of the concept of survival. Following the scientific principles of the ethological approach, we showed how tutors' aims and students' aims shifted over a period of time and how each group's aims interacted.

Two themes clearly emerged from our study: namely, that many tutors were concerned primarily with the technicalities of teaching the skills of literacy and their training usually emphasised this; and that the aims of the campaign were often a series of short-term pragmatic objectives, even though certain long-term aims were specified or implied in the BBC *Adult Literacy Handbook*. Nevertheless, although the scheme was initiated in a state of confusion so far as aims were concerned, the present study is a record of how these aims were modified and of how, in the face of students' reactions, criteria associated with the purposes of adult education came to the fore. In particular, the advantages of group tuition emerged strongly, as mirrors by which individual students were able to reassess their self-image, and the limitations of one-to-one tuition in achieving the objectives of adult education became clearer.

Consequently, through time, not only did the criteria for success change, but the priorities of individual criteria altered. Thus, through a process of classification and of reclassification of aims, a five-group schema of hypothetical criteria was produced. These five groupings were, in order of importance:

(i)   Affective personal achievements

(ii) Cognitive achievements

(iii) Enactive achievements

(iv) Socio-economic achievements

(v)   Affective social achievements.

Nevertheless, from the evidence in Chapters III to IX of their perceptions, given by tutors and students during two interviews well separated in time, and from samples of the students' written work, a re-ordered, amplified and scientifically more definitive list of criteria of achievement or success was devised: the emergent criteria.

(b) The emergent criteria

Perhaps the most important conclusion that can be asserted is that students did not primarily judge their success in terms of utilitarian objectives; they registered a feeling of increased confidence, often described as a feeling of being at ease within themselves. Because of this result, the order of importance of the five major groupings of criteria changed according to the frequency of 'confidence' factors within each grouping. The revised order of these groupings is, therefore:

(i)   Affective personal achievements
(ii)   Affective social achievements
(iii) Socio-economic achievements
(iv)   Cognitive achievements
(v)   Enactive achievements.

Though the evidence strongly supports the priority of affective achievements, there is far less certainty about the relative positions of each of the last three groupings because:

(a) the priority of each achievement depends largely on the individual student, and this is particularly true of the relative importance of the last three groupings to any specified student;
(b) the development of cognitive achievements is, as stated in the evidence given by students, more a matter of four or five years of tuition than of one or two years. It is therefore possible that if the period of this study had been extended, cognitive achievements might have become more important once the bed-rock foundation of student self-confidence was more firmly established.

However, cognitive achievements seemed to be more frequent and more important to students who were already in the upper bands of literacy ability. These students seemed to achieve confidence *through* cognitive achievement and the realisation of their expectation of cognitive progress proceeded *pari passu* with other achievements. Such cases were few in our sample population; the 'normal' student seemed to place cognitive achievement low in his scale of self-identified, experienced achievement.

On the assumption that improvements in self-image hinge upon *personal relationships*, as has been argued in the opening pages of this chapter, then the complete list of the constituent elements of the five groupings of emergent criteria of success, in order of importance, is as follows:

1 *Affective personal achievements*
   (a) a feeling of ease within oneself
   (b) an improvement in self-reliance
   (c) an improvement in assurance
   (d) a diminution of anxiety
   (e) a willingness to reconsider personal attitudes
   (f) an ability to assess evidence
   (g) an improvement in physical bearing
   (h) a willingness to evangelise
   (i) an increase in confidence associated with literacy skills:
       (i) a diminution of anxiety with regard to literacy;
       (ii) an increase in concentration during tuition;
       (iii) an expression of an expectation to succeed in the literacy skills;
       (iv) an expression of enjoyment in reading and writing.

2 *Affective social achievements*
   (a) better relationships through being willing to put forward one's point of view
   (b) better relationships within tuition groups
   (c) better relationships through sharing ideas about literacy
   (d) better relationships with all members of the family
   (e) better relationships through reading to children.

3 *Socio-economic achievements*
   (a) developing better relationships at the place of work
   (b) participation in civic duties such as:
       (i) participating in voluntary services
       (ii) accepting youth club leadership
       (iii) accepting committee membership duties
       (iv) improving parent-teacher liaison at children's school
       (v) accepting jury service
   (c) the assumption of greater responsibility at work
   (d) getting a better job in terms of personal satisfaction and interest
   (e) increasing the capability of re-entering the employment market
   (f) getting a job in terms of more pay.

4 *Cognitive achievements*
   (a) Reading achievements displaying an increase in:
       (i) word recognition skills
       (ii) sentence recognition skills
       (iii) comprehension skills

(iv) the ability to read informational texts

(v) the ability to read texts beyond the purely informational levels

(vi) the ability to read newspapers.

(b) Writing achievements showing an improvement in:

(i) the motor skill of writing

(ii) spelling

(iii) the ability to check spelling

(iv) the ability to take dictation

(v) the ability to complete commonly-used forms or questionnaires

(vi) the ability to write letters

(vii) the ability to write extended prose texts.

5 *Enactive achievements*

(a) regular attendance for tuition

(b) a movement from paired tuition at home to some form of group tuition

(c) use of reading skills, as shown by:

(i) reading to any member of the family

(ii) reading instructions at work

(iii) reading newspapers

(iv) reading books

(v) using the library service

(vi) finding directions from street signs or maps

(vii) using reading to exercise consumer choice

(d) use of writing skills, as exemplified by:

(i) completing forms, including cheques or payment slips

(ii) signing Christmas cards and addressing envelopes

(iii) writing free composition notes

(iv) using writing skills at work

(v) writing letters

(e) the public display of literacy 'tools': pens, pencils, etc.

(f) action to ameliorate physical deficiencies, such as acquiring spectacles

(g) general use of literacy skills in locating places from street signs or maps

(h) the use of communications relevant to consumer choice and payment systems

(i) an ability to evaluate the reliability of various communications media

(j) completion of homework assignments.

This list is based upon the philosophical criteria for judging achievement or success; in practice all the criteria are inter-related. Is it *not* in any way a prescription for ordering teaching methods nor is it a check list to be used to compare the progress of one student with another. All that is being stated is that any particular student is likely, from the evidence of our sample, to achieve some of these criteria of success.

The actual number of criteria of success that any student will wish to achieve will depend on his view of what level of self-image enables him to cope, to his satisfaction, with the majority of his practical, emotional and spiritual problems. It is thereby unlikely that any single criterion of success, couched in terms of any particular skill, will be an adequate measure of success for any student. What seems more probable is that a student will seek to achieve a sheaf* of criteria of success based entirely on individualistic preferences. The evidence strongly suggests that any grouping of criteria chosen by any individual will contain at least one of the most important of the criteria listed in the affective personal or social achievement domains, and that these are synonymous with the general aims of adult education.

Adult education is a healing process, but it cannot promise cures. If this proposition is acceptable, then it is understandable that the students in our sample and, over time, most of the tutors came to see that the literacy campaign was not a matter of skill-training but of adult education with special reference to literacy. It is therefore correct that a tutor should see success in ameliorative terms, principally in the improvement of self-image, and it is a pity that many tutors denigrated their achievements because of the lack of progress in the literacy skills.

Though all the criteria are inter-related, the centre of the activity is in the domain of adult education. Our concern has been the problem of the illiterate adult, and the evidence gathered was germane to that problem, but we may venture the hypothesis that any adult minority sub-group in which individuals think they have a particular problem in any specific skill will be best served within the domain of adult education. Because future initiatives of this kind may well take place, it is worth while examining in some detail the practical implications stemming from the philosophical stance described above.

(c) Practical implications

Though it is convenient to analyse the practical implications of the above theoretical argument in terms of the roles of organisers, tutors

---

* Mathematicians may care to read the source of this analogy as set out in the opening paragraphs of 'Continuously variable sets: algebraic geometry equals geometric logic', *Bristol Logic Colloquium 1973*, published by North Holland Press, 1975.

and students, the overall success of a literacy scheme depends fundamentally on the strength of the inter-relationships between these groups. The affirmation of this study is that a basic factor leading to correct relationships is an understanding by each group of the goals of a literacy scheme and an acknowledgement of the nature of the criteria of success.

Organisers

The principal problem facing organisers was whether to provide tutor/student facilities in a private home, to provide tutor/student facilities in a room under the supervision of a qualified and experienced tutor/organiser or whether to offer a class facility with a tutor and, say, five students.

It has been argued already that a student is more likely to be successful if he is a member of a group and that a student/tutor pairing in someone's home is psychologically restrictive and ineffective, except in special circumstances as, for example, the case of a student who is severely lacking in confidence because of some physical defect.

Furthermore the use of unqualified volunteers as tutors in an exercise which is firmly dependent on developing human relationships implies that such tutors require continuing support and guidance, which can be given only if a tutor/organiser is present and able to observe the developing social nuances. Such continuous availability is essential; sometimes the tutor/organiser will wish to switch a tutor from one student to another to avoid the growth of over-dependence or he will decide to leave a tutor with the same student for a longer period than is usual to build up confidence; sometimes he will recommend that the tutor uses a particular visual aid and he may even advise the tutor to try a different approach to solve a student's spelling problem.

We have suggested that at all times it is necessary for students to meet each other and to share problems if they are to succeed in engaging in the process of adult education. Similarly the tutors need regular opportunities to meet each other and, because of the presence of a professional tutor/organiser, they themselves may engage in the process of informal adult education on such occasions as the coffee-break period.

If the organisation is based on the principles outlined above, then the training schemes offered to volunteer tutors may be, first, extended beyond the limitations of an 8–10 hour preparatory course and, secondly, based on a more sensible estimate of what a normal volunteer tutor can learn without practical experience.

In the first case, the preparatory training scheme need not be based so much on the technicalities of literacy teaching; there will always be a professional tutor/organiser to help tutors as specific problems arise. Thus more attention may be given to the principles of adult education, with at least 50 per cent of the discussions centred on such principles.

Secondly, since the training of tutors in this type of tuition organisation is continuous, it is unnecessary to pack so much information into preparatory training schemes; the development of a volunteer's expertise will take place in the group where practice and principle may be related.

Tutors

At the end of the period of fieldwork, in July 1977, a tutor was asked to report on the progress of a student. In summary, the tutor replied:

> I am not really sure what sort of information you want . . . his spelling mistakes are almost as frequent, but much more logical than they used to be . . . he agreed that his reading is getting better although it is still quite a strain for him and he tires easily . . . his eye distorts 'then' into 'he' or 'here' into 'where' or perhaps 'her'. This sort of error throws out the sense of the sentence and then he thinks he has made a mistake with the longer words. . . . I fear he will never be able to 'scan read' because his eye gives his brain the wrong pictures, the same is probably true of his spelling – he can't see the right shape in his mind's eye. . . .
>
> However, we will press on. —— is very keen, he writes a diary and corresponds with lots of friends. . . .

Clearly this is an assessment from a *conscientious* tutor about a *keen* student; but the evidence of the letter suggests an over-emphasis on skill achievements as the criteria of success and, largely because the relationship is between only tutor and student, an under-emphasis of progress towards the criteria of success within the domain of adult education.

Moreover, one senses the tutor's isolation from other tutors in that she is unsure about the appropriate subject matter of a report on a student's progress. Similarly, one senses the student's isolation, since clearly he is a sharing-type of person as he writes to friends; on the basis of this letter and of an interview with the student, it is probable that he would enjoy meeting other students.

However, this letter is not quoted as a butt for criticism. It is a typical illustration of the predicament of tutors and students working in isolation, and even of some tutors and students working in groups where the tutor/organiser lacks the imagination to envisage, or the knowledge of, the principles of the practice of adult education. It illustrates the need for tutors continually to receive guidance and support from each other and from organisers. It demonstrates how much the counselling role of tutors and the criterion of confidence as a mark of success needs to be emphasised in training schemes. It also suggests that the fact that tutor and student are proven to be psychologically well-matched does not automatically result in a student's success; each party must know what the desired successes are.

Students

As more experience of interviewing was gained during the course of this study, it was realised how little the students required to be prompted. The interviewer became a mirror to which students directed their perceptions and saw reflected their own personality, their experiences and their hopes. So did tutors and organisers, who often said, 'We don't think of you as a person – if you see what we mean!' This experience, as well as the evidence of students' perceptions, leads to the conclusion that students sense the need for counselling as the most important ingredient in adjusting their self-image and, had they been able to formulate their needs in terms of adult education theory, they would have done so. It is only by accepting this that we can account for the persistence of the majority of students who knew that they were making very little or very slow progress in the skills of literacy. This was confirmed by the number of students who, when told that success could be correctly described in terms of the growth of confidence or the feeling of ease within oneself, positively beamed with delight.

For these reasons it seems probable that if tutors had really understood the criteria of success their initial – and developing – relations with their students would have been easier, and perhaps some 'dropouts' could have been avoided.

Most students, of their own volition or because of the public attention directed to illiteracy problems, expressed the view that their lack of skill in literacy was the cause of their perceived incompetence. In fact, most students needed to be reassured that their value as a human being was not to be measured in terms of literacy skills. This was the reason why so many students felt better when told the myth that two million adults were illiterate; if so many shared the disadvantage, what was wrong with them as one of so many?

Consequently when they appealed for help, their appeal was couched in terms of, for example, a wish to read to their children; when they had solely one tutor who took such a statement at face value as a demand for a technical skill, they were disappointed, for 'I wish to read to my children' also meant 'I feel that my wife treats me as an idiot because my son has to ask her all the time . . . I feel that I am being shouldered out of my rights as a father . . . I am letting down my wife and son . . . I am letting myself down!' Given those feelings, they required counselling and expertise from the tutor and support from fellow students, so that *whatever they gained in the skills was put to maximum use because of the generalised benefits of their experience of adult education*. Thus the establishment of the emergent criteria of success and the dissemination of this information among all the participants of literacy schemes should improve the quality of the schemes.

(d) Literacy and society

The Adult Literacy Campaign in the United Kingdom emerged from a conference held in 1973 and organised by the British Association of Settlements entitled 'A Right to Read'. David Hargreaves (1977), records that: 'Its (the BAS) advocacy was passionate, well-informed and skilful.' Through the influence of this pressure group, 'society' was persuaded to allocate the resources, human and financial, to provide a service for a section of the adult population whose needs had hitherto been largely ignored.

Out of this provision two major problems have emerged: first, that the passion which inspired the innovation of the national campaign will evaporate, largely because of the relatively small number of people willing to come forward for assistance, and, secondly, that future schemes will continue to be based upon skill training rather than being set within the context of adult education.

The strength of the adult education service in the United Kingdom lies in the variety of provision and, provided this characteristic remains, there should at all times be a place for adult illiterates, whatever their number.

Finally, adult education is only one of the means of increasing universal literacy. As the late Simeon Potter wrote:

The problem of illiteracy is not solved by compulsory schooling alone, if, as in Britain, many men's reading is limited to the gutter press, or, as in America, many people assume a 'mucker pose' and shun as affectation anything that suggests conscious refinement or ennoblement of life. Literacy is not a state, but a process: it cannot be finally guaranteed in any society. It involves hard toil in teaching the young and it demands the subsequent enlistment of every conceivable means of enlightening grown-ups – sound radio, television, cinema, theatre, press, museums, art gallery, public library, university extension and adult education. It is useless to teach the alphabet and the three Rs to young people and then turn them back into a society that remains stubbornly uncultured and unlettered. It is essential to fortify them continually against the insidious depravity of soul-destroying slogans; to train them to be wary of all absolutes and over-simplified either-or choices; to show them how to distinguish word from thing, and how to discriminate intelligently between facts and inferences and between inferences and value-judgements; to teach them to see how language really works in action; and to help them to recognise and respect life's fundamental loyalties.

(Potter, 1966, p. 186)

Afterword From literacy to basic education

The study reported in this book was completed in 1977 when the Adult Literacy Resource Agency was still operating. That means of financial support for adult literacy schemes came to an end in early 1978, being replaced by the Adult Literacy Unit, whose function is mainly advisory.

The cry now, however, is for a strategy of 'adult basic education' which will both continue the literacy work and build outwards from it into other fields of basic education. Attempts are being made in a number of places towards such an extension. Asked what they mean by 'basic education', most people seem to reply that they mean literacy, numeracy and 'life-skills' or 'coping-skills', a view that clearly owes something to the old elementary-school concept of the three Rs and also to a feeling that social inadequacy has a component of basic educational deficiency.

In that context, our present study has two clear messages. First, what the educational world has been calling literacy provision is often, in the perceptions of students, much more akin to what has been described as basic education. Progress in reading and writing was the proximate means towards affective achievements in personal and social life, towards the assertion of self-in-society, and achievements in the literacy skills themselves, even in their application to material situations, came lower in order of importance. Where success was most clearly felt, the students were receiving a general basic education and were not simply in classes for the three Rs.

Secondly, we have shown how the students in literacy tuition are a self-selected minority and it is then reasonable to ask how typical they are of the total constituency for a basic education programme. The evidence of this research is that they are more typical of that constituency than they are of a supposed constituency of 'illiterates'. Many were not, in the strict sense, illiterate. Their general or basic educational intentions became attached to the idea of literacy *because that was what was offered*. But how many others with basic educational needs were put off by this specific offering of literacy it is not possible to say. That some were so put off is suggested by the attitude of those who repudiated the label of 'illiterate'.

In sum, the literacy campaign became in effect a basic education programme because of the subtle interaction of the students' perceptions, including their self-perceptions, with their tutors' responsiveness. In a further programme of basic education a narrow concentration on skills, whether in the three Rs or in so-called 'life-skills', may be seriously misdirected if by that term is meant cognitive and enactive achievements, or behavioural objectives externally defined. The starting-point and the guidelines must be found in the potential students' own views of themselves.

Select bibliography

ADULT LITERACY RESOURCE AGENCY (1975–76, 1976–77, 1977–78) *Annual Reports*, HMSO, London.

ADULT LITERACY RESOURCE AGENCY (1977) *An Approach to Functional Literacy*, London.

ALEXANDER REPORT (1975) *Adult Education: the challenge of change*, HMSO, London.

BARROW, W. (1978) 'What Adults Read – Implications for Literacy' in *Perspectives on Adult Literacy*, United Kingdom Reading Association, pp. 33–36.

BAUCOM, K. L. (1978) *The ABCs of Literacy: lessons from linguistics*, International Institute of Adult Literacy Methods, Teheran.

BBC (1975) *Adult Literacy Handbook*, BBC Publications, London.

BERGER, P. L. (1966) *Invitation to Sociology*, Penguin, London.

BERGER, P. L., BERGER, B. and KELLNER, H. (1974) *The Homeless Mind*, Penguin, London.

BLOOM, B. S. *et al.* (1956) *Taxonomy of educational objectives – Handbook 1: Cognitive domain*, Longmans Green & Co., New York.

CHAMPION, A. (1975) 'Towards an Ontology of Adult Education' in *Studies in Adult Education*, Jones, H. A. (Ed.), 7 (1), pp. 16–33.

CHASE, S. (1954) *The Power of Words*, Harcourt Brace & Co., New York.

CHATFIELD, J. H. (1973) *Technology for Technicians – a study in relevance*, M.Ed. thesis (unpublished), University of Leicester.

CHOMSKY, N. (1973) 'Reading, Writing and Phonology' in *Readings in Applied Transformational Grammar*, Lester, M. (Ed.), 2nd ed., Holt, Rinehart & Winston, New York.

COOK, W. D. (1977) *Adult Literacy in the United States*, International Reading Association, Newark, Delaware.

CORDER, S. P. (1973) *Introducing Applied Linguistics*, Penguin, London.

EISNER, E. W. (1969) 'Instructional and Expressive Educational Objectives' in *Monograph No 3 on Curriculum Evaluation*, American Educational Research Association, Chicago.

ELSDON, K. T. (1975) *Training for Adult Education*, University of Nottingham.

GAGNÉ, R. M. (1966) *The Conditions of Learning*, Holt, Rinehart & Winston, New York.

GAGNÉ, R. M. (1967) 'Curriculum Research and the Promotion of Learning' in *Monograph No 1 on Curriculum Evaluation*, American Educational Research Association, Chicago.

GOLDBERG, S. (1951) *Army Training of Illiterates in World War II*, Teachers' College, Columbia, New York.

GUMPERZ, J. J. and HYMES, D. (1972) *Directions in Sociolinguistics: the ethnography of communication*, Holt, Rinehart & Winston, New York.

HARGREAVES, D. (1977) '*On the Move' – the BBC's contribution to the Adult Literacy Campaign in the United Kingdom between 1972 and 1976*, BBC Publications, London.

HARRIS, L. *et al.* (1970) *Survival Literacy Study*, National Reading Council, Washington DC.

HIRST, A. (1966) 'The man who teaches a word called HOPE', *The People*, 3 April, London.

HOGGART, R. (1957) *The uses of literacy*, Chatto & Windus, London.

HOLMES, J. (1976) 'Thoughts on Research Methodology' in *Studies in Adult Education*, Jones, H. A. (Ed.), 8 (2), pp. 149–163.

JELLIS, R. (1977) *Bird Sounds and their Meaning*, BBC Publications, London.

JONES, H. A. and CHARNLEY, A. H. (1978a) *Adult Literacy – a study of its impact*, National Institute of Adult Education (England and Wales), Leicester.

JONES, H. A. and CHARNLEY, A. H. (1978b) (Eds.) 'Literacy and Adult Education: the UK Experience' in *Literacy Discussion*, International Institute of Adult Literacy Methods, Teheran.

KEDNEY, R. J. (1976) 'Educational Objectives in Adult Literacy Provision' in *Studies in Adult Education*, Jones, H. A. (Ed.) 8 (1) pp. 1–14.

KEDNEY, R. J. (1978) 'Adult Literacy: Needs, Aims and Objectives' in *Perspectives on Adult Literacy*, United Kingdom Reading Association, pp. 17–31.

KOHL, H. (1974) *Reading, How to*, Penguin, London.

LESTER, M. (1973) (Ed.) *Readings in Applied Transformational Grammar*, 2nd ed., Holt, Rinehart & Winston, New York.

LIVERPOOL PROJECT (1976) *Where are they now?*, Liverpool Adult Literacy Project.

MAGER, R. F. (1962) *Preparing Instructional Objectives*, Fearon Publications, Palo Alto, California.

MEZIROW, J., DARKENWALD, G. G. and KNOX, A. B. (1975) *Last Gamble on Education*, Adult Education Association of the USA, Washington DC.

MORGAN, M. (1977) 'Adult Literacy in Taff-Ely' in *Links*, Evans, J. A. (Ed.), Links Association, Mid-Glamorgan, Wales.

MUSGROVE, F. (1977) *Margins of the Mind*, Methuen, London.

NORTHCUTT, N. (1975) *Functional Literacy for Adults: a status report of the Adult Performance Level Study*, Austin, Texas.

NORTHCUTT, N. (1976) 'Adult Performance Level' in *Materials and Methods in Continuing Education*, Klevins (Ed.), Klevens Publications, New York, pp. 273–281.

POTTER, S. (1966) *Language in the Modern World*, Penguin (Pelican), London.

POWELL, W. R. (1978) 'Levels of Literacy' in *Perspectives on Adult Literacy*, United Kingdom Reading Association, pp. 1–8.

RISMAN, A. (1975) 'Adult Illiterate Students' in *Studies in Adult Education*, Jones, H. A. (Ed.), 7 (2), pp. 142–149.

RUSSELL REPORT (1973) *Adult Education: a plan for development*, HMSO, London.

SCHUTZ, A. (1962–66) *Collected Papers*, Vols. I–III, Nijhoff, The Hague.

SNOW, D. W. (1976) *The Web of Adaptation*, Collins, London.

STICHT, T. G. *et al.* (1972) 'Determination of Adult Functional Literacy Skill Levels' in *Reading Research Quarterly*, 7 (3), pp. 424–465.

STICHT, T. G. (1975) (Ed.) *Reading for Working*, Human Resources Research Organisation, Alexandria Va., USA.

THORPE, W. H. (1974) *Animal Nature and Human Nature*, Methuen, London.

TINBERGEN, N. (1963) 'Aims and methods of ethology' in *Zeitschift zur Tierpsychologie*, vol. 20, pp. 410–433.

UNESCO (1965a) *Literacy as a Factor in Development*, Paris (Minedlit/3).

UNESCO (1965b) *World Conference of Ministers of Education on the Eradication of Illiteracy*, Final Report, Paris.

UNESCO (1972) *Third International Conference on Adult Education (Tokyo)*, Final Report, Paris (ED/MD/25).

UNESCO (1974) *Alphabétisation Fonctionelle et Apprentissage: Rendement Interne*, Paris.

UNESCO (1976) *The Experimental World Literacy Programme – A Critical Assessment*, Paris and London.

VILENSKY, L. D. and FRASER, B. J. (1977) 'Evaluation of a Vocational Curriculum', *Vocational Aspect of Education*, pp. 107–111.

WILDER, T. (1927) *The Bridge of San Luis Rey*, Longmans Green, New York and London.

Appendix A: Questionnaire of 25 phrases distributed to tutors

Instruction Sheet

In your opinion as a tutor, a tutor-trainer or an organiser:

Section A

1 Please classify, by placing a tick in the appropriate column, the degree of importance of each phrase as a *sign* of a student's 'achievement' or 'progress'. (A is the highest degree of importance.)

2 (a) Look down the A column and circle the tick √ which, in your opinion, is opposite the most important phrase as a sign of a student's progress.

   (b) Do the same for the B column

   (c) Do the same for the C column

   (d) Do the same for the D column

   (e) Do the same for the E column.

Section B

3 List the five most important phrases in Section A, by number, for each *stage* in a student's tuition.

Section A

No. of phrase	Phrase		Your coding				
			A	B	C	D	E
1	Regular attendance at classes	1					
2	General improvement in confidence and bearing	2					
3	Improvement in clarity of speech	3					
4	Improvement in range of spoken vocabulary	4					
5	Movement from a one-to-one learning situation to joining a group (even if individual teaching still takes place)	5					
6	Reading to his/her children	6					
7	Borrowing books from library	7					
8	Extending range of reading beyond information	8					
9	Reading information material	9					
10	Willingness to talk about his/her literacy problem	10					
11	Expression of expectation to succeed in reading and writing	11					
12	Diminution of anxiety (general)	12					
13	Joining more social groups	13					
14	Assumption of greater responsibility at work	14					
15	Better relationships with members of the family	15					
16	Increase in comprehension skills	16					
17	Increase in word recognition skills	17					
18	Ability to take dictation	18					
19	Ability to check spelling	19					
20	Ability to write a letter	20					
21	Ability to read newspapers	21					
22	Increase in the period of concentration during tuition	22					
23	Diminution of anxiety with regard to literacy	23					
24	Getting a better job in terms of more pay	24					
25	Getting a better job in terms of personal satisfaction and interest (not necessarily better paid)	25					

(Please remember to ring the most important tick in each column)

Section B

I have been advised that the order of importance of the phrases in Section A may depend on the *stage* of the student's tuition; in order to cover this point I have suggested three stages.

Using the numbers of the phrases in Section A, will you please enter what *you* feel are the five most important phrases, in order, for each stage.

Stage	Order				
	1 (most important)	2	3	4	5
1 After a few weeks' tuition					
2 After one year's tuition					
3 At the end of the student's course					

What was the main reason given by student for applying for help in reading/writing/spelling? (Please delete if not applicable.)

Reason (his/her words if possible)...

....

Other phrases which you think describe achievement and which you think I should take into account:

(a) ....

(b) ....

(c) ....

....
Name of tutor/trainer/organiser

Appendix B: Additional criteria of success as suggested by tutors to Section B of Appendix A

The following 169 replies were received to the question which asked for 'Other phrases which you think describe achievement and which you think I should take into account'.

1. (a) ability to 'attack' words not in student's vocabulary
   (b) ability to find meaning of unknown words
   (c) ability to write legibly
2. (a) ability to join in conversation with peers
   (b) ability to discuss topics
3. (a) keeping one step ahead of own children learning to read
   (b) being able to sleep at night
   (c) being able to write out own cheques
   (These were given by tutor as *actual* examples)
4. (a) social competence
   (b) better citizen
5. offhand attitude of employer (DHSS) should be mitigated
6. ability to clearly express thoughts in writing (*sic*)
7. (a) assumption of more respect from society
   (b) more confidence in forming *new* friendships
   (c) improvement of performance in hobbies' skills
8. Comment: 'I think as a tutor one's concept of achievement could vary from pupil to pupil (*sic*), i.e. one would feel some points were more important to one pupil than another. This form seems to generalise too much'
9. (a) feeling of 'being as good as anyone else'
   (b) knowing that one can cope with any reading or writing work alone

10   (a)   acceptance of him/herself by others before and after tuition
     (b)   willingness to help others as he/she has been helped
11   (a)   voluntarily to bring forward work done at home
     (b)   able to fill in a questionnaire form, etc., without fear
     (c)   able to admit to his/her difficulty to others beside the tutor
12   (a)   to understand word building and to write sounding-out words
     (b)   to find how to spell a word, i.e. dictionary
     (c)   to read and write more independently, i.e. self-help
13   (a)   acknowledgement of need – 'I know I want practice and have got to work at it'
     (b)   improvement in companionable domestic skill – 'I shall write out the shopping list instead of my wife'
     (c)   use of cursive handwriting instead of capitals
14   buying books or aids at own suggestion, e.g. 'On the Move' workbook
15   (a)   perhaps their being able to grasp their *own* problem as part of a larger very common problem – to blame not themselves but the society which abandoned their problem for so long and limited their real potential
     (b)   to attain a greater tolerance and understanding of different customs, beliefs and others' problems, through their reading
16   (a)   ability to see and assess his own improvement
     (b)   ability to relate what is learnt to everyday experiences
17   desire for further education (e.g. O levels)
18   (a)   regular attempt and/or completion of homework
     (b)   interest in words beyond present skills
19   (a)   ability to cope with everyday situations, e.g. shops, public transport
     (b)   to have a sense of achievement
     (c)   to realise ambitions regarding career
20   gradually to overcome aggressive feeling to society in general
21   Comment: 'I have no experience in answering any questions (X is my first student) – as yet it is beyond my knowledge'
22   ability to fill in time-sheets and such like forms for work
23   (a)   to help his son when he starts school
     (b)   to join an English class later to improve grammar and construction
24   (a)   diminish personal anxiety
     (b)   draw his/her own pension
     (c)   teach her daughters to read
25   (a)   ability to understand and fill in forms
     (b)   greater fluency in writing
     (c)   ability to make quality comparisons when shopping

26 (a) ability to use a dictionary
    (b) confidence in completing official forms
    (c) to be independent of other people
27 (a) to realise literacy problems are quite common
    (b) following or developing hobbies via reading/writing
    (c) new understanding of grammatical skills
28 (a) ability to help children with school work
    (b) ability to understand instructions regarding safety and medicines
    (c) ability to shop confidently and unaided
29 (a) ability to use a dictionary
    (b) habitual use of a good dictionary
    (c) economy of self-expression
30 (a) ability to shop in a 'supermarket'
    (b) willingness to do homework
31 (a) eagerness to work beyond the prescribed time
    (b) enrolment for further education
    (c) confidence to assist fellow students
32 reading books for pleasure
33 recognition of patterns in spelling
34 (a) taking an *interest* in reading and word formation
    (b) expression of actual progress already made
35 getting literacy problem into perspective
36 (a) ability for the eye to go before the voice when reading
    (b) ability to read with expression and not just read each word separately
    (c) confidence to work with other students – testing spelling, etc.
37 (a) to have confidence in the tutor
    (b) to have a friendly relationship with the tutor
Comment: 'I feel you should place more emphasis on the tutor-student relationship'
38 (a) ability to remember simple grammatical rules
    (b) gaining confidence with other adults apart from tutors and family
39 the development of a more enquiring mind
40 (a) to progress further in education, i.e. O level English
    (b) to join recreational classes at college
    (c) to help generally in the community, i.e. youth work, voluntary social work, etc.
41 (a) to assume role of leader/organiser in social setting
    (b) ability to become himself a tutor of illiterates
42 (a) ability to read menu posted in canteen or cafe
    (b) ability to read simple posters on 'works' notice board
    (c) eligibility to drive a car and find way by maps

43   (a)   recognition of initial letters
     (b)   non-reversal of letters
     (c)   reading with a child
44 ability to understand and respond to punctuation marks
45 ability to use punctuation marks correctly
46 ability to write more quickly and confidently
47   (a)   an increased awareness of various aspects of literacy
     (b)   constructive attitude towards the problem
     (c)   active curiosity overcoming personal shame
48 ability to enjoy the written word
49 lessening of dependence on tutor – move to self-learning
50 ability to verbalise experiences, however simple
51 joining a class instead of one-to-one tuition
52   (a)   ability to express ideas in writing, to undertake creative writing
     (b)   to take examinations giving qualifications
53   (a)   ability to write one's name
     (b)   ability to fill in forms
     (c)   familiarity with the order of the alphabet (to be able to use dictionaries and telephone directories)
54   (a)   ability to generalise
     (b)   using context to work out meaning
     (c)   going back and correcting without prompting
55   (a)   ability to see and correct mistakes unaided
     (b)   ability to generalise and see patterns
     (c)   ability to read for context and meaning rather than just trying sounds to letters
     (d)   Comment: '(tutor's own) increasing confidence that he, as an individual, might, one day, make some sense out of it all'
56 ability to read and write
57   (a)   student's persistent attempts to work by himself
     (b)   student's pleasure and awareness of increments of success
58   (a)   ability to generalise – some general rules and apply them in practice
     (b)   to read for meaning rather than mechanically
59 feeling more confident at work

Appendix C: Additional criteria of success

Recorded by Georgina Ingleby in her enquiry conducted in 1976 (under the direction of Dr. Margaret Peters of the Cambridge Institute of Education).

To the question 'What level of achievement would you count as success for your student?' 26 out of 37 tutors responded, as follows:

1   The ability to stay ahead of her infant son
2   Able to communicate by using the written word
3   'If he wrote a decent, acceptable, moderately well-spelt and grammatical letter. Would also like him to have some understanding of the basic structure of language and even *enjoy* reading and writing'
4   A reading age of 9–10 years for academic success (brain damaged)
5   O level English
6   Just being able to recognise necessary words
7   When he is satisfied with his results
8   Able to read, write and spell to a satisfactory standard
9   When he can write from dictation
10   Able to read independently and tackle new long words. A reader for pleasure rather than just *Daily Mirror/The Sun* fluency. A sliding scale of success would have to be adjusted every few months
11   Ability to understand and write simple English
12   Ability to write reports (on trade union meetings) and make short notes on, e.g. operation of machinery, spell confidently, use cursive script, not capitals
13   To read with fluency an easy newspaper
14   Short-term aim – to read a book (possibly Ladybird)

15 Improvement in spelling of words which follow a simple rule. Also common and useful words

16 Too early to say

17 To be able to pick up any piece of printed matter and read it fluently. To be able to write clearly and correctly

18 Able to compete with others at day release

19 Better writing ability, i.e. upright instead of sloping in all directions

20 Read reasonably difficult book fluently, without hesitation; write fluently

21 Success achieved so far (a) confidence to address a stranger, (b) first letter ever written in her life, (c) expressed pleasure in reading

22 Ability to apply for a specific job. Success in reading away from the tutor-student situation. Fluent reading, autonomy

23 Able to express ideas on paper, correct spelling of *basic* words, coherently, readably

24 Keep one step ahead of her children's reading. Ability to cope with official forms and letters; read and use recipes, read horoscopes, 'agony' column. Write letters to school and family

25 When he can regard print in a positive way, not something to be feared

26 Initially – self-motivation – to *want* to read. Having mastered the reading skills, to then use them in everyday life as well as read for pleasure

Index